Russian Grammar for Beginners
Textbook and Workbook Included

Supercharge your Russian with essential lessons and exercises

Also available:

Russian Short Stories for Beginners (https://geni.us/russianstories)

TABLE OF CONTENTS

Introduction

When learning any language, grammar definitely comes up as the most challenging—and boring—part. Russian is no different. Unfortunately, grammar is not something that can just be brushed off as an afterthought.

You simply cannot skip learning grammar if you truly want to become proficient. It doesn't work that way, and there are no shortcuts. If you want to be able to express yourself in Russian using clear and precise language, you need to build a solid foundation in Russian grammar.

This book is here to help you. In the lessons in this book, we will lay down the rules in Russian grammar and provide you with lots of examples, clarifications, and exercises.

Practice Your Russian Listening Skills and Pronunciation

A key to success in language learning is to get a good grasp of pronunciation at the beginning of your lessons. This requires constant listening practice. With this book's audio accompaniment, you will get a headstart in your listening comprehension as well as hone your pronunciation straight off the bat.

Each lesson and exercise contains audio narrated by a native Russian speaker. By listening to the audio and reading the written text at the same time, you will be able to connect how a word and sentence looks with how it sounds when spoken in actual Russian conversations.

Embedded Grammar Workbook

There is no need to buy a separate workbook to help you practice the grammar points you learn. We have integrated hundreds of different types of exercises into the book. This way, you will be able to cement your learning through taking the quizzes after each grammar lesson and you will be able to assess your progress as you go along.

Build a Learning Habit

This book also aims to help you build a learning habit that will help you sustain your Russian learning even if your motivation wanes as you go along. You'll find that the book is divided into 20 lessons, with one lesson meant to be tackled each day. After

20 days of studying consistently everyday, you will have formed a learning habit that will ultimately help you achieve your learning goals.

Russian Grammar, Simplified

Russian grammar is already complicated—we don't need to make it even more complex. So in this book, you'll notice that we use the simplest yet thorough explanations. We do not want to burden you with wordy explanations and unnecessary jargon. Instead, in this book we explain Russian grammar in a way that makes it easily digestible and easy to grasp.

We have put a lot of effort into this book so that it will be most useful to your Russian language learning journey. We certainly hope that it will help you build the strong grammar foundation you need to eventually reach fluency in Russian.

Thank you very much.

My Daily Russian Team

Important! The link to download the AUDIO FILES is available at the end of this book. (Page 215)

Lesson 1: How to Introduce Yourself in Russian?

It is always daunting to initiate a conversation with a native if you've just started learning a foreign language. But luckily there are basic Russian phrases that help you easily introduce yourself. Even if your Russian doesn't let you hold deep and long conversations yet, these simple expressions are more than enough to lay the beginning of a great friendship.

Initiating a conversation

If you want to get acquainted with a Russian, there are two ways you can start a conversation depending on how formal you want to be.

In an informal setting (for example, in a bar or at a party), you can approach a person by saying:

Listen to Track 1 (Reminder: you can download the audio from the link available at the end of the book, page 215)

Привет!	*Hi!*
Меня зовут Джейк.	*My name's Jake.*
Очень приятно.	*Nice to meet you.*

In a formal setting (for example, in the university or at a conference), you can start a conversation with these words:

Listen to Track 2

Здравствуйте!	*Hello!*
Меня зовут Джейк.	*My name is Jake.*
Приятно познакомиться.	*It's a pleasure to meet you.*

Listen to Track 3

If it is a Russian who starts the conversation, they may ask you what your name is. In Russian, it is:

Как тебя зовут?	*What's your name? (informal)*
Как Вас зовут?	*What is your name? (formal)*

(If we translate this question literally, it means "How are you called?")

You already know how to answer this question:

Listen to Track 4

Меня зовут Джейк.	*My name's Jake.*
Очень приятно.	*Nice to meet you.*

OR

Меня зовут Джейк.	*My name's Jake.*
Приятно познакомиться.	*It's a pleasure to meet you.*

To express a friendly attitude, Russians can also use phrases like **Рад познакомиться** (masculine) / **Рада познакомиться** (feminine) or **Рад знакомству** (masculine) / **Рада знакомству** (feminine).

Talking about yourself

During a conversation, a Russian may ask you some questions. For example, where you are from or what your occupation is. Even if they don't ask, you can take the initiative and spice up the conversation with some details about yourself.

Listen to Track 5

Я из (your native country or city)... – *I am from...*

For example:

- **Я из Великобритании.** – *I am from Great Britain.*
- **Я из Англии.** – *I am from England.*
- **Я из США** (pronounced Se-Shi-Ah). – *I am from the United States.*
- **Я из Канады.** – *I am from Canada.*

If you don't know how to correctly pronounce your country in Russian, just name it as it is pronounced in English. Russians will understand.

Listen to Track 6

Мне (age) лет. – *I am ... years old.*

For example:

- **Мне тридцать лет.** – *I am thirty years old.*
- **Мне двадцать два года.** – *I am twenty-two (years old).*
- **Мне сорок один год.** – *I am forty-one (years old).*

Please note that if the age (cardinal number) ends in one, two, three, or four, Russians use the word **год / года**. For all other ages, they use **лет**.

Listen to Track 7

Я (occupation). – *I am a (occupation).*

For example:

- **Я учитель.** – *I am a teacher.*
- **Я студент.** – *I am a student.*
- **Я программист.** – *I am a coder.*
- **Я юрист.** – *I am a lawyer.*

Interestingly, you need neither a verb nor an em dash in this sentence (the em dash is used in Russian in place of a missing verb) because the subject is a pronoun.

Listen to Track 8

Я работаю в (place). – *I work at/in (place).*

For example:

- **Я работаю в школе.** – *I work at a school.*
- **Я работаю в большой компании.** – *I work in a big company.*
- **Я работаю на себя.** – *I am self-employed.*

When indicating a place of work, Russians usually use preposition **в** followed by a noun in the prepositional case. The preposition **на** is used less frequently, usually for big places such as a plant, a factory, a market, etc.

For example:

- **Я работаю на фабрике**. – *I work in a factory.*

Listen to Track 9

Я учусь в... – *I'm studying at...*

For example:

- **Я учусь в университете.** – *I'm studying at the university.*

The use of the preposition **в** is the same as in phrases about work.

Listen to Track 10

Я изучаю русский язык уже (duration) – *I have been learning Russian for (duration).*

For example:

- **Я изучаю русский язык уже полгода.**
  – *I've been learning Russian for half a year already.*
- **Я изучаю русский язык уже пять лет.**
  – *I've been learning Russian for five years already.*

The use of cardinal numbers (years) is the same as in the phrases about age.

Listen to Track 11

Я учу русский потому что (reason). – *I am learning Russian because (reason).*

Natives often want to know why you learn Russian. Maybe you need it for work or education, or you've found your true love in Russia and are learning Russian to be able to have a heart-to-heart with your darling. Or maybe you are a polyglot, and Russian is your new goal. The expression **Я учу русский, потому что (reason)**, which means "I am learning Russian because (reason)," helps you talk about your real motives.

For example:

- **Я учу русский потому что моя жена — россиянка.**
  – *I'm learning Russian because my wife is Russian.*
- **Я учу русский потому что у меня бизнес в России.**
  – *I'm learning Russian because I've got a business in Russia.*
- **Я учу русский потому что он мне нравится.**
  – *I'm learning Russian because I like it.*

Listen to Track 12

Я увлекаюсь (hobby). – *I like (hobby).*

And now, the cherry on top: your hobbies! Telling people about your passions helps them better understand what kind of personality you are. There are a few ways you can talk about your hobbies:

Example:

- **Я увлекаюсь футболом и рыбалкой.**
  – I like (am passionate about) soccer and fishing.
- **Мои хобби — чтение и археология.**
  – My hobbies are reading and archeology.
- **В свободное время я люблю готовить и играть в настольные игры.**
  – In my free time, I like to cook and play board games.
- **Мне нравится танцевать румбу и кататься на мотоцикле.**
  – I like dancing rumba and riding my bike.

Let's put these phrases together and see what we get:

Listen to Track 13

Привет, меня зовут **Ник**. Я **студент**. Мне **22 года**. Я из **Великобритании**. Я учу русский язык уже **год**. Я учу русский, потому что **хочу жить и работать учителем в России**. Мне нравится **работать с детьми**. Я также увлекаюсь **чтением и теннисом**.

Hi, my name's Nick. I am a student. I am 22. I am from Great Britain. I have been learning Russian for a year already. I am learning Russian because I want to live and work in Russia as a teacher. I love working with children. I also like reading and tennis.

Wow! That's a huge beginning! Now you have an easy-to-follow self-introduction scheme. Just replace the bold text with your personal information and test it out whenever you happen to talk to a native.

We've got more exciting content for you. Please check out the exercises for this topic on the next page.

TIME TO PRACTICE!

Exercise 1 - Imagine you are in Russia travelling by bus. The person that is sitting next to you is a native of your age. How would you start a conversation and introduce yourself? Use the prompts below.

Привет! – *Hi!*   - *ПРИВЕТ*

Меня зовут...– *My name is...*   - *Меня зовут fatима*

Я из... – *I'm from...*   - *Я из angliti*

А как тебя зовут? – *And what's your name?*   - *меня зовут nerian*

познакомитьуа

Приятно познакомиться.– *It's a pleasure to meet you.* -

Exercise 2 - Put these phrases in the correct order to create a dialogue:

3 Меня зовут Даша. – *My name's Dasha.*   -

9 И я рада знакомству.–*Nice to meet you too.*   -

2 Здравствуйте! – *Hello!*   -

откуда

7 Откуда вы? – *Where are you from?*   -

4 А вас как зовут? – *What's your name?*   -

8 Приятно познакомиться. – *Nice to meet you.*   -

5 Меня зовут Питер. – *My name's Peter.*   -

6 Я из Англии. – *I'm from England.*   -

1 Доброе утро! – *Good morning!*   -

Exercise 3 - A native asks you why you are learning Russian. Write your answer.

Native: Почему вы учите русский? *(Why are you learning Russian?)*.

You: ... - *Я учите русский потому что*

Exercise 4 - Your new Russian friend asks you about your hobbies. What would you answer? Try using different phrases for describing your hobbies.

Native: Чем ты увлекаешься?*(What's your hobby?)*

You: ... -

Exercise 5 - Write a brief self-introduction. Mention your age, native country, occupation, how long you've been learning Russian and your hobbies.

Answers

Exercise 1

You: Привет! Меня зовут Алекс. Я из США. А как вас зовут?

Native: ...

You: Приятно познакомиться.

Exercise 2

— Доброе утро!

— Здравствуйте!

— Меня зовут Питер. А вас как зовут?

— Меня зовут Даша.

— Приятно познакомиться.

— И я рада знакомству. Откуда вы?

— Я из Англии.

Exercise 3

Native: Почему вы учите русский? (*Why are you learning Russian?*).

Example:

You: Я учу русский, потому что я хочу поехать в путешествие по России.

Exercise 4

Native: Чем ты увлекаешься?

You: Мне нравится заниматься боксом и путешествовать. OR: Я люблю заниматься боксом и путешествовать. OR: Мои хобби — бокс и путешествия.

Exercise 5 (example)

Здравствуйте, меня зовут Чарли. Я врач. Мне 30 лет. Я из Канады. Я учу русский два года. Мне нравится путешествовать и учить иностранные языки.

Lesson 2: Russian Alphabet

Learning Russian starts with its alphabet. If your mother language doesn't belong to the group of Slavic languages, chances are that the Cyrillic script the Russians use will blow your mind. However, every cloud has a silver lining. Russian pronunciation is very easy and, in fact, it has a lot fewer rules than, say, English or French. We are here to help you out with understanding Russian letters and their pronunciation.

But first...

A few Interesting historical facts about Russian and its alphabet

- Another word for the Russian alphabet is **азбука** (azbuka). It was created from the first two letters ("аз" and "буки") of the oldest known prototype of the Russian alphabet, **глаголица** (Glagolitsa).

- Glagolitsa (or the Glagolitic alphabet) was artificially created by two brothers, Cyril (827-869 AD) and Methodius (826-885 AD), who were Byzantine scholars and monks. They were looking for a way to spread Christianity across the Slavic nations, which didn't have their own writing system at that time. For this purpose, they developed Glagolitsa for translating the Bible and other Christian texts for Slavic people.

- In the 10th century, the disciples of Cyril and Methodius "upgraded" Glagolitsa, making it more similar to the Greek script and named it **Cyrilitsa** after their "guru" Cyril.

- Russia (then a part of Kievan Rus') was Christianized soon after that (988 AD). The Cyrillic alphabet became the base for the Old Church Slavonic language, the only written language used by Russian people until the 17th century.

- The Russian emperor Peter the Great (1672-1725) realized the need for a civil written Russian language, which could be used for science, diplomacy, education and all other non-religious purposes. He offered a new alphabet for the civil Russian language based on the Moscow dialect.

- The next (and last) language reform was initiated in 1918 when four letters were removed from the alphabet.

- Belarusian and Ukrainian languages are the closest to Russian. They are both also developed from the Old Church Slavonic language.

The Russian alphabet

The alphabet Russians use today consists of 33 letters:

Listen to Track 14

- 10 vowels: **а, е, ё, и, о, у, ы, э, ю, я.**
- 20 consonants: **б, в, г, д, ж, з, к, л, м, н, п, р, с, т, ф, х, ц, ч, ш, щ.**
- One semivowel: **й.**
- Two letters that modify hardness/softness: **ъ** and **ь.**

Listen to Track 15

Russian letter	Handwriting	Name	Similar sound in English	Example
Аа		а [a]	*father*	**а**пельсин (*orange*) за**па**д (*west*)
Бб		бэ [bə]	**b**ack	**б**ассейн (*pool*) **б**лины (*Russian pancakes*)
Вв		вэ [və]	**v**ine	**в**ишня (*cherry*) **в**ино (*vine*)
Гг		гэ [gə]	**g**ood	**г**од (*year*) **г**олубь (*dove*)
Дд		дэ [də]	**d**o	**д**орога (*road*) **д**ом (*house*)
Ее		е [jə]	**y**ellow	**Е**вропа (*Europe*) б**е**рег (*coast*)
Ёё		ё [jo]	**yo**ghurt	**ё**лка (*firtree*) тяж**ё**лый (*heavy*)
Жж		жэ [zhə]	*plea**s**ure, mea**s**ure*	**ж**елезо (*iron*) **ж**елтый (*yellow*)
Зз		зэ [zə]	**z**ero, **z**oo	**з**акат (*sunset*) **з**емля (*land, ground*)

Ии		и [i:]	*n**ee**d*	**и**стор**и**я (*history*) Ир**и**на (*a woman's name*)
Йй		и краткое [i: ˈkratkəjə]	*bo**y**, jo**y***	поко**й** (*peace*) **й**огурт (*yoghurt*)
Кк		ка [ka]	*can, **k**ept*	**к**онь (*horse*) **к**источка (*paint brush*)
Лл		эл [əl]	*l**amp*	**л**ожка (*spoon*) **л**ето (*summer*)
Мм		эм [əm]	*m**any*	**м**ашина (*car, vehicle*) **м**ир (*world*)
Нн		эн [ən]	*n**ever*	**н**ож (*knife*) **н**ебо (*sky*)
Оо		о [o]	*m**o**re*	**о**зеро (*lake*) м**о**л**о**к**о** (*milk*)
Пп		пэ [pə]	*p**en*	**п**ирог (*cake*) **п**ерсик (*peach*)
Рр		эр [ər]	*rolled r*	**р**абота (*work*) **р**ука (*hand*)
Сс		эс [əs]	*s**oft*	**с**такан (*glass*) **с**нег (*snow*)
Тт		тэ [tə]	*t**ap*	**т**уман (*fog*) **т**рава (*grass*)
Уу		у [u]	*l**oo**k*	**у**лыбка (*smile*) б**у**мага (*paper*)
Фф		эф [əf]	*f**ence*	**ф**абрика (*factory*) **ф**иолетовый (*violet*)
Хх		ха [ha]	*Lo**ch** Ness*	**х**леб (*bread*) **х**удожник (*painter*)

Цц		цэ [tsə]	*fits*	**ц**арь (*tsar*) **ц**веток (*flower*)
Чч		че [chə]	**ch**ess	**ч**еловек (*man, person*) ту**ч**а (*cloud*)
Шш		ша [sha]	**sh**arp	**ш**кола (*school*) Ма**ш**а (*a woman's name*)
Щщ		ща [shcha]	*similar to* **sh**eep	**щ**енок (*puppy*) ро**щ**а (*grove*)
Ъъ		твёрдый знак [ˈtˈviordɨj znak]	*"The hard sign". It makes the preceding consonant hard.*	под**ъ**езд (*entrance*) суб**ъ**ект (*subject*)
Ыы		ы [ɨ]	*slightly similar to s**i**t*	м**ы** (*we*) б**ы**стро (*quickly*)
Ьь		мягкий знак [ˈmiahkeej znak]	*"The soft sign". It makes the preceding consonant soft.*	день (*day*) плать**е** (*dress*)
Ээ		э [ə]	*let*	**э**кология (*ecology*) **Э**стония (*Estonia*)
Юю		ю [ju]	**u**se	**ю**г (*south*) **ю**бка (*skirt*)
Яя		я [ja]	**ya**rd	**я** (*I*) мен**я** (*me*)

Please note:

- Vowels **и**, **я**, **ю**, **е** and, of course, **ь** make the preceding consonant soft: листья [lˈisˈtˈja], мять [mˈatˈ], любить [lˈubˈitˈ].(Please note that the symbol ' after the consonant indicates softness of this consonant.)

- Letters **ь** and **ъ** don't begin Russian words: пла**ть**е, ес**ть**, клас**ть**.
- The letter **ы** can begin words, but none of them are native Russian (most of them are words denoting geographic locations): **Ы**нда-Сылла世.
- The letter **ё** is rarely used in modern Russian. Today, many words are written with **е** instead of **ё**: тяж**е**лый, деш**е**вый, ж**е**лтый.

Russian pronunciation tips

- Don't worry if you cannot pronounce Russian sounds, for example **р** (the rolling r). Practice makes perfect. It is a really difficult sound that many Russian kids cannot say until they are five or six years old. Even some adult Russians have difficulties with **р**.
- It can be confusing for a non-Russian-speaking person that some Russian letters look like Latin letters but have an absolutely different sound. For example, В is [v], not [b]; and Х is [h], not [ks]. It is because Russian adopted elements from different languages including Greek and Latin. A good tip here is not to compare Russian with other languages and to read as much Russian text as possible.

Listen to Track 16

- We pronounce Russian words almost in the same way as they are written, but not exactly. For example, when it comes to central dialects (which form the phonetic core of the language), we pronounce **о** as **о**, **а** as **а**, **е** as **е** and **я** as **я** only when they are stressed.

  For example, as in these words: д**О**ждь, с**А**д, сн**Е**г, м**Я**ч.

Listen to Track 17

- In the unstressed position, we pronounce **о** and **а** as "uh" (something in between [a] and [ə]) and **е** and **я** as "ee":

  молок**О** — muh-luh-ko

  сараф**А**н — suh-ruh-fan

  телеф**О**н — tee-lee-fon

  боев**О**й — buh-yee-voy

  мяч**И** (pl.) — mee-chee

  Such vowel reduction affects the language in such a way that the sounds "а" and "и" become dominant. For this reason, linguists call this phenomenon акание ("akanye") and икание ("eekanye").

- When you just begin to learn Russian, the best way to get used to its alphabet and pronunciation is to listen to Russian speakers reading some Russian text while following it with your eyes. Your brain will adjust very quickly.

We are always here and ready to help if you have a question or any difficulties with Russian pronunciation. Also, you can try out the exercises we developed to help you learn the Russian alphabet in an easy and fun way.

TIME TO PRACTICE!

Exercise 1—Divide this cloud of letters into 4 columns:

ё н г ш и п р щ з э

я ч с й ц ф ы у к е м х о л

д ъ в а ж б т ь ю

Consonants	Vowels	Modifiers	Semivowel

Exercise 2—How would you pronounce these sounds:

В in **в**илка

    a. As [b]   b. As [v]   c. As [və]   d. A s [v']

С in **с**ахар

    a. As [k]   b. As [s]   c. As [əs]

Х in **х**итрый

    a. [h']   b. [h]   c. [ks]

Я in **я**ркий

    a. [ja]   b. [a:]   c. ['a]

Exercise 3—Choose the corresponding sounds in English for these Russian letters:

Щ

    a. Like "sh" in "shorts"

    b. Like "sh" in "sheet"

    c. Like "sch" in "school"

Х

    a. Like "h" in "happy"

    b. Like "ch" in "Loch Ness"

    c. Like "kʃ" in "luxury"

И
> a. Like "i" in "bit"
>
> b. Like "ee" in "feed"
>
> c. Like "y" in "boy"

Ю
> a. Like "u" in "use"
>
> b. Like "u" in "mute"
>
> c. Like "u" in "minute"

Exercise 4—Choose the correct pronunciation for these words (stressed letters are capitalised):

берегА (pl.):
> a. bee-ree-ga
>
> b. bie-rie-ga

зОлото:
> a. zo-luh-to
>
> b. zo-luh-tuh
>
> c. zo-lo-tuh

компьЮтер:
> a. kuhm-pyu-teer
>
> b. kom-pu-ter
>
> c. kuhm-pyu-ter

янтАрь:
> a. yan-tar'
>
> b. yeen-tar
>
> c. yeen-tar'

Answers

Exercise 1

Consonants	Vowels	Modifiers	Semivowel
н г ш п р щ з ч с ц ф к м х л д в ж б т	ё и э я ы у е о а ю	ъ ь	й

Exercise 2

В: [v'] / С: [s] / Х: [h'] / Я: [ja] /

Exercise 3

Щ — like "sh" in "sheet". / Х — like "ch" in "Loch Nes". / И — like "ee" in "feed". / Ю — like "u" in "use".

Exercise 4

берегА: a) / зОлото: b) / компьЮтер: a) / янтАрь: c)

Lesson 3: Numbers - How to Count in Russian

From prices in shops and phone numbers to buses and addresses, numbers surround us wherever we go. So if you want to enjoy full freedom while in Russia, you need to learn how to use the Russian numerical system. Similarly to English, Russian numbers fall into cardinal and ordinal. In this post, we will tell you about these two types of number and how to use them for counting.

Cardinal numbers in Russian

Put simply, cardinal numbers help us to tell the quantity of something. In comparison with other languages, Russian cardinal numbers are very intuitive and simple to create. The only difficult thing about them is probably the pronunciation (but we will help you out with that as well).

Russian numbers 0—10:

Listen to Track 18

English	Russian	Russian pronunciation
zero	Ноль	nol'
one	Один	əˈdeen
two	Два	dva
three	Три	Tree
four	Четыре	chəˈtyrə
five	Пять	pyat'
six	Шесть	shest'
seven	Семь	syem'
eight	Восемь	vosyem'
nine	Девять	dyevyat'
ten	Десять	dyesyat'

For example:

У моей сестры есть две кошки, а у меня пять попугаев.

My sister has two cats, and I have five parrots.

Try to say the numbers from zero to ten and backwards several times.

Russian numbers 11—19

Numbers from 11 to 19 are easy to form by adding **-надцать** (and slightly changing the stem for some numbers):

Listen to Track 19

English	Russian	Russian pronunciation
eleven	один**надцать**	ə'deenatsyt'
twelve	две**надцать**	dveenatsyt'
thirteen	три**надцать**	treenatsyt'
fourteen	четыр**надцать**	cheetyrnatsyt'
fifteen	пят**надцать**	peetnatsyt'
sixteen	шест**надцать**	shysnatsyt'
seventeen	сем**надцать**	seemnatsyt'
eighteen	восем**надцать**	vaseemnatsyt'
nineteen	девят**надцать**	deevyatnatsyt'

Russian numbers 20 and onward

To form a compound number, you need to take a round number (for example, twenty) and add any unit from 1 to 9, which you already know. Here's how it works:

Listen to Track 20

English	Russian	Russian pronunciation
twenty	два**дцать**	dvuhtsyt'
twenty-one	двадцать один	dvuhtsyt' uhdeen
twenty-two	двадцать два	dvuhtsyt' dvuh
twenty-three	двадцать три	dvuhtsyt' tree
twenty-four	двадцать четыре	dvuhtsyt' cheetyree
twenty-five	двадцать пять	dvuhtsyt' pyat'
twenty-six	двадцать шесть	dvuhtsyt' shest'
twenty-seven	двадцать семь	dvuhtsyt' syem'
twenty-eight	двадцать восемь	dvuhtsyt' vosyem'
twenty-nine	двадцать девять	dvuhtsyt' dyevyat'
thirty	три**дцать**	treetsyt'

20 (**двадцать**) and 30 (**тридцать**) are formed by adding **-дцать.** However, not all tens in Russian form in the way **двадцать** and **тридцать** are.

Here's how we create them.

Russian tens 40—90

Numbers five, six, seven and eight form their tens by adding **-десят.** Numbers 40 and 90 don't fit this logic, so you need to memorise their unique forms: **сорок** and **девяносто**.

Listen to Track 21

Numbers	Russian	Russian pronunciation
40	сорок	soruhk
50	пять**десят**	peedeesyat
60	шесть**десят**	shysdeesyat
70	семь**десят**	syemdeesyat
80	восемь**десят**	voseemdeesyat
90	девяносто	deevyanostuh

Russian hundreds, thousands and onward

One hundred in Russian is **сто** (stoh).

However, unlike in English, some other hundreds are created not by saying the number of hundreds (like three hundred, for example), but as separate unique words.

Hundreds from 500 to 900 are formed similarly, by adding **-сот** to a number. Other hundreds are exceptions and need to be memorised:

Listen to Track 22

Number	Russian	Russian pronunciation
200	двести	dvyestee
300	триста	treestuh
400	четыреста	cheetyreestuh
500	пятьсот	peetsot
600	шестьсот	shyssot
700	семьсот	seemsot
800	восемьсот	vuhseemsot
900	девятьсот	deevyatsot
1,000	тысяча	tysyachuh
1,000,000	миллион	meeleeon
1,000,000,000	миллиард	meeleeuhrd

Saying large cardinal numbers

Look at how we say large numbers in Russian. Keep in mind that words **тысяча**, **миллион**, and **миллиард** impact the number's gender and change themselves by number and case. We promise to get into the nitty-gritty of it in a later chapter.

Listen to Track 23

- 85 — восемьдесят пять
- 126 — сто двадцать шесть
- 547 — пятьсот сорок семь
- 1,205 — (одна) тысяча двести пять
- 5,450 — пять тысяч четыреста пятьдесят
- 6,763,421 — шесть миллионов семьсот шестьдесят три тысячи четыреста двадцать один
- 7,654,323,936 — семь миллиардов шестьсот пятьдесят четыре миллиона триста двадцать три тысячи девятьсот тридцать шесть

Note: If we have only one thousand, million or billion, we can omit the word **один/одна**.

How about halves?

Sometimes we deal with a not quite even number of things. How do we say halves in Russian?

Listen to Track 24

- 0.5 is **половина** (or **пол-**)
- 1.5 is **полтора**
- 2.5 (and onward) is formed by adding **с половиной**.

All of these types of halves put a noun into the genitive case.

For example,

- **Пол-яблока** – *half an apple*
- **Полтора метра** – *one and a half meters*
- **Два с половиной года** – *two and a half years*

Ordinal numbers in Russian

We need ordinal numbers to describe an object's order or position. And ... the Russian ordinal numbers come with a secret too. Not only do they decline by case, but they also get altered by gender and number (sorry for this unavoidable tautology), behaving just like adjectives.

In this post, we will introduce you to the basic form of Russian ordinal numbers (nominative case, masculine, singular) and get back to the declension principles in a separate chapter.

Russian ordinal numbers 1—10

Listen to Track 25

English	Russian	Russian pronunciation
first	Первый	pyervyy
second	Второй	ftuhroy
third	Третий	tryeteey
fourth	Четвертый	cheetvyortyy
fifth	Пятый	pyatyy
sixth	Шестой	shystoy
seventh	Седьмой	seed'moy
eighth	Восьмой	vas'moy
ninth	Девятый	deevyatyy
tenth	Десятый	deesyatyy

Russian ordinal numbers 11—19

Listen to Track 26

Numbers from 11 to 19 create ordinal numbers by discarding **ь** and adding the ending **ый**: одиннадцат**ый**, двенадцат**ый**, тринадцат**ый**, четырнадцат**ый**, пятнадцат**ый**, шестнадцат**ый**, семнадцат**ый**, восемнадцат**ый**, and девятнадцат**ый**.

Russian ordinal numbers: 21 and onward

When we create ordinal numbers out of compound cardinal numbers, for example 26 or 247, only the last digit becomes ordinal, and the rest of the number stays cardinal (the same as it is in English).

Listen to Track 27

For example:

- двадцать **шестой** – *twenty-**sixth***
- двести сорок **седьмой** – *two hundred forty-**seventh***

Russian ordinal numbers 20—90

Tens from 20 to 90 form ordinal numbers in a similar way (by adding **–ый or -ой)**, but 40 is still an exception:

Listen to Track 28

English	Russian	Russian pronunciation
twentieth	Двадцат**ый**	Dvuhtsuhtyy
thirtieth	Тридцат**ый**	Treetsuhtyy
fortieth	сороковой	Suhruhkovoy
fiftieth	Пятидесят**ый**	Peeteedeesyatyy
sixtieth	шестидесят**ый**	Shysteedeesyatyy
seventieth	Семидесят**ый**	Seemeedeesyatyy
eightieth	восьмидесят**ый**	vuhs'meedeesyatyy
ninetieth	Девяност**ый**	Deeveenostyy

Russian ordinal numbers: hundreds, thousands and onward

Ordinal hundreds in Russian are formed by adding **-сотый**:

Listen to Track 29

English	Russian	Russian pronunciation
100th	Сотый	Sotyy
200th	двух**сотый**	Dvookhsotyy
300th	трех**сотый**	Tryokhsotyy
400th	четырех**сотый**	Cheetyryokhsotyy
500th	пяти**сотый**	Peeteesotyy
600th	шести**сотый**	Shysteesotyy
700th	семи**сотый**	Seemeesotyy
800th	восьми**сотый**	vuhs'meesotyy
900th	девяти**сотый**	Deeveeteesotyy
1,000th	тысячный	Tyseechnyy
1,000,000th	миллионный	Meeleeonnyy
1,000,000,000th	миллиардный	Meeleeuhrdnyy

Conclusion

Russian numbers aren't something easily digestible, but regular practice conquers all. So we invite you to check out the exercises we prepared for this lesson. Also, bookmark this guide and get back to it when needed. Learning Russian numbers doesn't stop here, since we mentioned already that they decline by case, and there's a lot you need to learn about them. So make sure you read the section on Russian number declension to bring your Russian counting skills to perfection.

TIME TO PRACTICE!

Exercise 1 - Complete the sequences by filling the gaps with missing numbers:

1. Один, ____, ____, четыре, ____, шесть, семь, ____, ____, ____ .
2. Двенадцать, ____, ____, пятнадцать, ____, ____, ____, девятнадцать, ____ .
3. Двадцать восемь, ____, ____, тридцать один, ____, ____, тридцать четыре.

Exercise 2 - Write these numbers with words in Russian:

43, 49, 57, 92, 148, 395, 1,490   - _____

Exercise 3 - Create Russian numbers with halves using the prompt:

0.5 + час = полчаса

1. 0.5 + пицца =   - _____
2. 0.5 (половина) + кровать =   - _____
3. 1.5 + километр =   - _____
4. 10.5 + час =   - _____

Exercise 4 - Create ordinal numbers:

15, 24, 40, 56, 90, 136, 400, 657, 700 - _____

Answers

Exercise 1

1. Один, два, три, четыре, пять, шесть, семь, восемь, девять, десять.

2. Двенадцать, тринадцать, четырнадцать, пятнадцать, шестнадцать, семнадцать, восемнадцать, девятнадцать, двадцать.

3. Двадцать восемь, двадцать девять, тридцать, тридцать один, тридцать два, тридцать три, тридцать четыре.

Exercise 2:

Сорок три

Сорок девять

Пятьдесят семь

Девяносто два

Сто сорок восемь

Триста девяносто пять

Тысяча четыреста девяносто

Exercise 3

1. Полпиццы
2. Половина кровати
3. Полтора километра
4. Десять с половиной часов

Exercise 4

Пятнадцатый

Двадцать четвертый

Сороковой

Пятьдесят шестой

Девяностый

Сто тридцать шестой

Четырехсотый

Шестьсот пятьдесят седьмой

Семисотый

Lesson 4: Word Order in the Russian Language

Word order. If these two words make you sick every time you start to learn a new language, relax for now... In Russian, the word order is fairly flexible. Although you can always go with the classic **Subject—Verb—Object** order, Russian grammar allows you to arrange these three in virtually any possible combination.

For example, if an English speaker has only one way to say that *a boy ate an apple* (without making it passive), a Russian speaker has at least six ways to say the same thing:

Listen to Track 30

1. Мальчик съел яблоко.
2. Мальчик яблоко съел.
3. Яблоко съел мальчик.
4. Яблоко мальчик съел.
5. Съел мальчик яблоко.
6. Съел яблоко мальчик.

And no, we aren't having a combinatorics lesson — it's just Russian word order, baby!

This amazing flexibility doesn't, however, mean we can mindlessly lump words together in a sentence. There's still a thing or two you should know about the word order in Russian. Let's look at how it works in practice.

What makes word order in Russian so flexible?

In the Russian language, grammatical cases mark the role of every word in the sentence by modifying it using specific endings (inflections). Since the function of a word is tied to its grammatical form, the word order becomes less important. Wherever you put the word, it retains its grammatical features, and everyone understands what you are talking about.

Actually, you have even more reasons to be happy while learning Russian:

Listen to Track 31

1. In Russian, there are no articles (neither definite nor indefinite). How do we know, for example, whether someone means a random apple or a particular one? We know it from the context.

2. Russian speakers often drop pronouns if the context is clear. For example:
   - **(Я) Хочу спать (Спать хочу).** – *I want to sleep.*

3. In the present tense, the verb "to be" is always omitted (replaced with a dash):
   - **Изучение языков – мое хобби.** – *Learning languages is my hobby.*
   - **Мой брат – врач.** – *My brother is a doctor.*

Note: a dash isn't needed when the subject is a pronoun. Like here:

- **Он врач.** – *He is a doctor.*

Where do we put certain parts of speech in Russian?

Nouns and verbs

As we already know, nouns and verbs in Russian can trade places in a sentence, and the phrase remains grammatically correct. Yet, the reversed word order does have a strong semantic effect. In other words, rearranging nouns and verbs helps create the effect of definite and indefinite articles that Russians simply don't have.

Listen to Track 32

Verb + noun = indefinite article effect:

- **Звонил мужчина** – *A man called.*

Noun + verb = definite article effect:

- **Мужчина звонил** – *The man called.*

Do you remember the phrase *"A boy ate an apple"* we used in the very beginning? Although we can create up to 6 combinations of subject, verb, and object while translating it into Russian, their meaning will vary slightly. The reason is that the Russians put the word they want to emphasize at the beginning. Compare:

Listen to Track 33

- **Сергей любит пиццу.** – *Sergey loves pizza.*
- **Любит Сергей пиццу.** – *Sergey does love pizza.*
- **Пиццу Сергей любит.** – *Pizza is what Sergey loves.*

Adjectives and nouns

Listen to Track 34

We normally use adjectives and participles before nouns:

- **красное яблоко** – *A red apple*
- **маленький ребенок** – *A small child*
- **тяжелая сумка** – *A heavy bag*

If the adjective is used after the noun, it acts as a predicate:

- **Яблоко красное.** – *The apple is red.*
- **Ребенок маленький.** – *The child is small.*
- **Сумка тяжелая.** – *The bag is heavy.*

Since adjectives and participles in Russian are marked with case endings (it is called declension), it is always clear which adjective/participle modifies which noun. Like adjectives, participles can go both before and after nouns:

- **Песня, написанная им, стала очень популярной.** OR
  Написанная им песня стала очень популярной.
  The song written by him became very popular.

Adverbs

Listen to Track 35

By default, most adverbs are put before adjectives and verbs they modify.

- **Я обычно** встаю в семь часов. – *I **usually** get up at seven o'clock.*
- Мой брат **очень** общительный. – *My brother is **very** sociable.*

Still, adverbs can change their default position to emphasize other parts of speech. Please, compare these Russian phrases with their English translation and see how the meaning changes as the adverb **только** "travels" the sentence.

- **Только** сегодня я прочитал эту книгу. – ***Only*** *today, I have read this book.*
- Сегодня **только** я прочитал эту книгу. – *Today,* ***only*** *I have read this book.*
- Сегодня я **только** прочитал эту книгу. – *Today, I have* ***only*** *read this book.*
- Сегодня я прочитал **только** эту книгу. – *Today, I have read* ***only*** *this book.*

Forming questions in Russian

There are three ways of forming questions in the Russian language.

Listen to Track 36

1. Using question words (interrogative adverbs)

   For example:
   - **Где** ты живешь? – ***Where*** *do you live?*
   - **Как** тебя зовут? – ***What***'s *your name?*
   - **Сколько** тебе лет? – ***How old*** *are you?*

2. Using question intonation

   Yes/no questions in Russian are formed in a truly magical way. The word order remains similar to that of a statement; we only put the question mark at the end and pronounce the phrase with question intonation.

   For example:
   - **Ты поедешь** в Россию следующим летом. – *You are going to go to Russia next summer.*

3. Putting a verb before a noun

   The inverted word order is less common in Russian questions. It is usually used with the conjunction ли to form a question whereby we express our doubts about the positive response.

   For example:
   - Захочет **ли** он поужинать с нами? – *Will he want to have dinner with us?*

Word order in negative sentences

Listen to Track 37

- To negate a verb, use the particle **не**. For example:
  Я **не** люблю читать фантастику. – *I **don't** like reading fiction books.*

- If you want to answer the question with "no," use the particle **нет**:
  Ты голоден? **Нет**. – *Are you hungry? **No, I'm not**.*

- **Нет** also means that something is not present. For example:
  Его здесь **нет**. – *He is **not** here.*
  У меня **нет** с собой документов. – *I have **no** documents with me.*

- Unlike in English, double negatives aren't just proper, but mandatory in Russian.
  For example:
  Я **никогда не** был в Китае. – *I have **never** been to China.*
  Здесь **никто не** живет. – ***Nobody** lives here.*
  Вы **ничего не** понимаете. – *You understand **nothing**.*

How word order impacts meaning

As you already know, in Russian, you can use the subject, verb, and object in any possible combination. If the phrase is taken out of context, such rearrangement won't change the meaning dramatically. However, if there is a particular context, rearrangement of the subject, verb, and object does change the meaning.

You may have already heard that a sentence has two logical parts: a theme and a rheme. The theme provides information that is already known, and the rheme introduces new information. Since Russians put logical emphasis on the rheme, you can confuse them if you move new information closer to the beginning. Let's look at how it works.

Listen to Track 38

- Год назад я **написал книгу**.
  The accent is on the fact that I wrote a book.

- Год назад я написал книгу **о своих путешествиях**.
  The accent is on the fact that I wrote a book about my travels.

- Книгу о своих путешествиях я **написал год назад**.

  The accent is on the fact that I wrote it a year ago.

- Год назад о своих путешествиях я написал **книгу**.

  The accent is on the fact that I described my travels in the form of a book, and not, say, a blog.

- Год назад книгу о путешествиях написал **я**.

  The accent is on the fact that it was me who wrote the book about travels a year ago.

After English with its strict word order, the Russian language may seem a little bit chaotic to some people. That's absolutely normal. Your mind needs some time to get used to making logical accents at the end of a sentence, as well as building questions and double negatives properly. In other respects, the Russian word order is a joy to practice.

TIME TO PRACTICE!

Exercise 1 - Create sentences putting the words in the right order:

1. речку вчера Никита с ездил друзьями на. *(Yesterday Nikita went with friends to the river.)*

_____

2. школе чтобы Майкл русский работать в учит московской. *(Michael is learning Russian to work at a Moscow school.)*

_____

3. теннис вечер с будем мы друзьями играть весь сегодня в. *(My friends and I are going to play tennis all night.)*

_____

4. еда мороженное детей любимая самая. *(Ice cream is the favorite food of children.)*

_____

5. картина а столом висит лежит кот под над столом. *(Under the table is a cat, and above the table hangs a picture.)*

_____

Exercise 2 - Translate these sentences and phrases into Russian trying to adjust the word order to the emphasis being made:

1. A boy came.   - _____
2. The boy came.   - _____
3. My brother is an artist.   - _____
4. My brother is the artist.   - _____
5. The tea is strong.   - _____
6. There is a chair near the bed. - _____
7. The chair is near the bed.   - _____

Exercise 3 - Adverbs normally go before adjectives and verbs they modify. Correct the wrong word order in these sentences:

1. Макс любит слушать громкую очень музыку. *(Max likes to listen to very loud music.)*

_____

2. Я беру с собой всегда в путешествие книгу. *(I always take a book with me when traveling.)*

_____

3. Поскорей мне хочется закончить делать домашнее задание и пойти гулять. *(I want to finish my homework and go for a walk as soon as possible.)*

_____

4. Будет хорошая завтра погода. *(Tomorrow will be good weather.)*

_____

Exercise 4 - Create questions in Russian using the beginnings suggested. Learn to pronounce them with a rising intonation:

1. Где...?   - _____
2. Ты...?   - _____
3. Почему...? - _____
4. Как...?   - _____
5. Будет ли...? - _____

Exercise 5 - Identify a theme and rheme in these sentences. Translate them into English accordingly:

1. В следующем году я отправлюсь в путешествие по России.

_____

2. В путешествие по России я отправлюсь в следующем году.

_____

3. В следующем году в путешествие по России отправлюсь я.

_____

Answers

Exercise 1

1. Вчера Никита ездил с друзьями на речку. 2. Майкл учит русский, чтобы работать в московской школе. 3. Мы с друзьями будем сегодня весь вечер играть в теннис. 4. Мороженое – самая любимая еда детей. 5. Под столом лежит кот, а над столом висит картина.

Exercise 2

1. Пришел мальчик. 2. Мальчик пришел. 3. Мой брат – художник. 4. Художник – мой брат. 5. Чай крепкий. 6. Возле кровати стоит стул. 7. Стул стоит возле кровати.

Exercise 3

1. Макс любит слушать очень громкую музыку. 2. Я всегда беру с собой в путешествие книгу. 3. Мне хочется поскорей закончить делать домашнее задание и пойти гулять. 4. Завтра будет хорошая погода.

Exercise 4

1. Где живет твоя семья? 2. Ты говоришь по-русски? 3. Почему тебе нравится учить иностранные языки? 4. Как будет "сочинение" по-русски? 5. Будет ли сегодня урок по грамматике?

Exercise 5

1. Next year I am going to travel around Russia.
2. I am going to travel around Russia next year.
3. The one who will travel across Russia next year will be me.

Lesson 5: Asking/Telling the Time and Date in Russian

Although asking the time is becoming rarer and rarer now that everybody has smart gadgets with them, time never disappears from our speech. Like any other language, Russian breathes time in all its variations, and every learner has to grasp how to ask and tell the date and time in Russian.

How do we ask the time in Russian?

Listen to Track 39

In the Russian language, we've got two different expressions to ask the time: **"Который час?"** and **"Сколько времени?"**

They both mean *"What time is it?"* and can be used in formal and informal conversation alike. However, when talking to strangers, you shouldn't forget to use some polite expressions such as:

- **Извините (простите), не подскажете, который (сейчас) час?**
  Excuse me, could you please tell me the time?

- **Скажите, пожалуйста, сколько времени?**
  Please tell me, what time is it?

That was the easiest part. Here comes the hardest one – understanding the answer and telling the time when someone asks us about it.

How do we tell the time in Russian?

There are two ways to tell the time in Russian. The first one (digital clock style) is easier. The second one (analogue clock style) is more complex. However, you have to understand both ways, as you never know which way the person you ask about the time will use.

1. Telling the time in a "digital" style

If you already know the cardinal numerals in Russian (the first 60 are enough), telling the time will be a breeze. You just need to say the number of hours followed by the number of minutes.

Listen to Track 40

For example, *it's 18:35 now.*

In Russian, it will be **восемнадцать часов тридцать пять минут.**

Please note that in this kind of phrase, you need to put the words **часы** (*hours*), **минуты** (*minutes*) or **секунды** (*seconds*) into the genitive case.

Just remember these three forms:

- **часы** (nominative case, plural) → **часов** (genitive case, plural)
- **минуты** (nominative case, plural) → **минут** (genitive case, plural)
- **секунды** (nominative case, plural) → **секунд** (genitive case, plural)

Such a precise, "military" style of telling the time is more suitable for formal communication. In everyday conversations, we usually do the following:

- Omit the words **часов** and **минут** and simply say **восемнадцать тридцать пять.**
- Use the 12-hour time and specify the time of the day using the words **утра, вечера, дня,** or **ночи** only when it's crucial for understanding. For example: 18:35 (or 6:35 p.m.) becomes **шесть тридцать пять вечера.**
- From 4 a.m. to 11 a.m., we use **утра.** From 12 p.m. to 4 p.m., we say **дня.** From 5 p.m. to 11 p.m., we say **вечера.** From 12 a.m. to 3 a.m., we use the word **ночи.**
- When it's 1 a.m. or 1 p.m., we substitute the numeral "one" with the word **час.**

This is how it works:

Listen to Track 41

Time in 24-hour format	Russian (conversational)
8:00	восемь (часов) утра
8:45	восемь сорок пять утра
20:45	восемь сорок пять вечера
15:00	три (часа) дня
03:00	три (часа) ночи
01:25	час двадцать пять ночи
23:25	одиннадцать двадцать пять вечера
13:00	час дня
01:00	час ночи
00:00	двенадцать ночи OR полночь
12:00	двенадцать дня OR полдень

2. Telling the time in the "analogue" style

To master this style, you need to learn these words first:

Listen to Track 42

- **четверть** – *quarter past*
- **без четверти** – *quarter to*
- **половина** – *half an hour to*
- **пол** – *half an hour to*
- **без** – *without*
- **почти** – *almost*
- **ровно** – *exactly*

A. Quarters

Listen to Track 43

- When it's 15 minutes past something, we can say the time this way:

пятнадцать минут + next hour (ordinal numeral in the genitive case)

OR

четверть + next hour (ordinal numeral in the genitive case).

- When we have a quarter to something, we say:

без пятнадцати + next hour (cardinal numeral, nominative case)

OR

без четверти + next hour (cardinal numeral, nominative case)

For example:

Listen to Track 44

Time in 24-hour format	Russian	Russian (version 2)
8:15	пятнадцать минут девятого	четверть девятого
12:15	пятнадцать минут первого	четверть первого
00:15	пятнадцать минут первого	четверть первого
16:15	пятнадцать минут пятого	четверть пятого
19:15	пятнадцать минут восьмого	четверть восьмого
12:45	без пятнадцати час	без четверти час
13:45	без пятнадцати два	без четверти два

Please note:

You can use the words **утра, дня, вечера,** or **ночи** when it's crucial to specify the time of the day or when you talk about future events.

B. Halves

Listen to Track 45

Like in English, we use **половина** or **пол-** (half) for 30 minutes. However, unlike in English where we say "half past something", in Russian, we put the emphasis on the hour that will be next:

половина + next hour (ordinal numeral, genitive case)

Please, keep in mind that **пол-** is a prefix, so if you use it, it becomes the first part of the ordinal numeral that means the next hour.

For example:

Time in 24-hour format	Russian	Russian (version 2)
8:30	половина девятого	Полдевятого
12:30	половина первого (дня)	полпервого (дня)
00:30	половина первого (ночи)	полпервого (ночи)
16:30	половина пятого (дня)	полпятого (дня)
04:30	половина пятого (утра)	полпятого (утра)

C. Minutes

Listen to Track 46

* When we have 1 to 29 minutes past something, here is how to say it in Russian:

number of minutes + **минута/минут/минуты** + next hour
(ordinal numeral, genitive case)

For example:

Time in 24-hour format	Russian
8:01	одна минута девятого
10:21	двадцать одна минута одиннадцатого
11:22	двадцать две минуты двенадцатого
16:20	двадцать минут пятого

For foreigners, it can be hard to understand when to use **минута** and when **минут** or **минуты**. Follow this simple rule:

- o 1 or 21 minutes – use **минута**
- o 2-4 or 22-24 – use **минуты**
- o 5 and more (except 21-24) – use **минут**

- When the minutes are from 31 to 59, we use the word **без**:

  без + number of minutes (cardinal numeral, genitive case) + **минут** (optional) + next hour (cardinal numeral, nominative case).

  Note: If the next hour is 1 a.m. or 1 p.m., don't forget to substitute **один** with the word **час**.

For example:

Listen to Track 47

Time in 24-hour format	Russian
8:40	без двадцати девять
10:50	без десяти (минут) одиннадцать
11:55	без пяти двенадцать
16:35	без двадцати пяти (минут) пять
23:59	без одной минуты полночь
12:50	без десяти час
00:40	без двадцати час

Listen to Track 48

We know … it looks and sounds overwhelming now. But it will get easier and easier as you practice. By the way, there's good news for you! When it's 5 to 1 minutes to something, you can round it up using **почти** (*almost*):

- **почти десять** – *it's almost 10 a.m. (9:57)*
- **почти час** – *it's almost 1 p.m. (12:58)*

Now we are ALMOST finished with telling the time. We just have to try actually using it in real communication.

Alternative ways to indicate the time

1. Simplified way

The easiest scheme to indicate the time is successive reading of numerals, meaning hours and minutes:

Listen to Track 49

- **Девять двадцать пять** – *9:25*
- **Восемнадцать сорок пять** – *18:45*

2. Words connected with the time

Listen to Track 50

- **Сейчас (*now*)** – refers to an action taking place at the moment of speaking:
  Сейчас 6 часов утра! Прекратите шуметь! – *Now it's 6am! Stop making noise!*
  N.B. While answering the question "**Который час**?" (*What time is it?*) the word "**сейчас**" is often omitted.
  So, answering the question about time we will say "7:30" (instead of "**Сейчас 7:30**").

- **Скоро (*soon*)** – meaning something will take place in the near future:
  Скоро будет 8 часов, откроются магазины. – *Soon it will be 8, and the shops will open.*

- **Почти (*almost*)** – something will take place very soon:
  Уже почти 5 часов. До конца рабочей смены осталось 15 минут.
  It's almost 5 o'clock. There are only 15 minutes remaining until the end of the working shift.

- **Ровно (*exactly*)** – demonstrates the exact moment of time:
  Ровно в 19:00 свет погаснет и начнётся представление.
  At exactly 19:00 the light will go off and the performance will start.

- **Примерно / Около (*around/about*)** – these are synonyms indicating an approximate time the particular action:

  Я видел его примерно в 3 часа дня. – *I saw him at about 4pm.*

  Около 11 часов я услышала странные звуки из-за двери.

  Around 11 o'clock I heard strange noises from behind the door.

- **В (*at*)** – the preposition, indicating the exact time:

  Урок начинается в 14:05. – *The lesson starts at 14:05.*

3. Expressions with the word время (*time*)

Listen to Track 51

- **Пришло время ... (*The time has come to ...*)**

  Я долго ждала. Пришло время серьезно поговорить.

  I have waited too long. The time has come to talk seriously.

- **Не время ... (*It's not the right time to...*)**

  Не время идти в гости – уже 23:00.

  It's not the right time to go on a visit — it's already 23:00.

- **Опоздать (*to be late*)**

  Полицейские опоздали – грабитель сбежал.

  The policemen were late — the robber ran away.

- **Время покажет (*Time will tell*)**

  Время покажет, кто был прав. – *Time will tell who was right.*

- **Время от времени (*From time to time*)**

  Время от времени я перечитываю эти правила. – *From time to time I reread these rules.*

Using time expressions in sentences

Now that you know how to tell the time in Russian, you need to practice using it in different life situations. Have a look at these examples and pay attention to the **prepositions** we use with the time expressions.

Listen to Track 52

- Stating the time – no preposition:

  Когда в Москве восемь утра, в Нью-Йорке еще только час ночи.

  When it's 8 a.m. in Moscow, it's still only 1 a.m. in New York.

- Telling the exact time when the event happens – preposition **в**:

  Занятия в школе начинаются **в** полдевятого утра и заканчиваются **в** два часа дня.

  School begins at half past eight in the morning and is over at two in the afternoon.

  Метро закрывается **в** полночь. – *The subway closes at midnight.*

- Events that happen after a certain time – preposition **после** (requires genitive case):

  Она сможет присоединиться к нам **после** семи.

  She can join us after seven o'clock.

- Events that happen by a certain time – preposition **к**:

  Сегодня потеплеет **к** полудню. – *It will get warmer by noon today.*

- Approximate time – preposition **около**:

  Он придет **около** шести. – *He will come around six o'clock.*

Listen to Track 53

Other time expressions you should remember:

- **на рассвете** – *at dawn*
- **утром** – *in the morning*
- **в полдень** – *in the afternoon, at noon*
- **вечером** – *in the evening*
- **на закате** – *at dusk*
- **ночью** – *at night*

How do we ask and tell the date in Russian?

Listen to Track 54

1. Date without event (in the abstract)

Let's imagine, you want to find out today's date without referring to any event. For example, you've forgotten what's on the calendar. This is how to ask about it in Russian:

- **Какое сегодня число?** (*What's the date today?*)

To answer this question, you need to:

1. Know the date.
2. Put the date (ordinary numeral) into the nominative case, neutral gender, singular. The ending will be **-ое** (or **-е** for number three).
3. Put the month (months in Russian are nouns of the masculine gender) into the genitive case, singular. The ending will be **-а / -я**.

It only seems difficult. Here's how easy it is in reality:

1. Let's imagine, it's the 4th of June today.
2. **Четыре** (four, cardinal numeral) → **четвертый** (ordinary numeral, nominative case, masculine, singular) → **четвертое** (ordinary, nominative, neutral, singular).
3. **Июнь** (June, noun, masculine, nominative, singular) → **июня** (genitive, singular).

So, the answer is:

- Сегодня четверт**ое** июн**я**. – *Today is the fourth of June.*

Please note that, unlike in English, we use lowercase for the months in Russian.

In the same way, you can ask about **вчера** (*yesterday*), **позавчера** (*the day before yesterday*), **завтра** (*tomorrow*) or **послезавтра** (*the day after tomorrow*).

For example:

- Какое число было **вчера**? **Вчера** было треть**е** июн**я**.
  What was the date yesterday? It was the 3rd of June.

- Какое **завтра** число? **Завтра** (будет) пят**ое** июн**я**.
  What will the date be tomorrow? It will be the 5th of June.

Now, how about the year? It's highly unlikely that you (or anybody) will forget it... but maybe someday you will travel into the past (or even cooler, into the future), and you'll need to ask about it. Then say:

- **Какой сейчас год?** – *What year is it?*

In Russian, we tell the year in the same way as you name the four-digit number in math. All digits in the nominative case. The last digit turns into the ordinary numeral (if it's zero, the last two digits):

- **две тысячи двадцатый год** – *2020*
- **одна тысяча девятсот восемдесят пятый** – *1985*

Telling the full date

Easy. Just name the date in nominative case followed by month and year (last digits) in the genitive.

Listen to Track 55

- Сегодня четверт**ое** июн**я** две тысячи двадцат**ого** год**а**. – *Today is the fourth of June, 2020.*

2. Date + event

Listen to Track 56

Now let's imagine you need to find out the date when an event happens. Then we start our question with **Когда...?** (*When...?*) or **Какого числа...?** (*On what date...?*).

To answer, we need to put both the date and the month in the genitive case. The date gets an ending **-ого** (or **-его** for number three). The month will end with **-а** / **-я**.

For example:

- Какого числа приезжает твой брат? Десят**ого** март**а**.
  On what date is your brother coming? On the 10th of May.

- Когда у твоей жены день рождения? Двадцать треть**его** ноябр**я**.
  When is your wife's birthday? It's on the twenty-third of November.

Please note:

двадцать треть**его** ноябр**я**

When a date is a two-digit number (like 23 or 31), we put only the ones into the genitive case and leave tens as they are (in the nominative case).

For your convenience, we have created a table where you can find Russian ordinal numbers and months already put in nominative and genitive cases so that you can practice telling the date in Russian with ease.

Listen to Track 57

Date	Ordinal numbers, Nominative	Ordinal numbers, genitive	Months, genitive
1	Первое	первого	января
2	Второе	второго	февраля
3	Третье	третьего	марта
4	Четвертое	четвертого	апреля
5	Пятое	пятого	мая
6	Шестое	шестого	июня
7	Седьмое	седьмого	июля
8	Восьмое	восьмого	августа
9	Девятое	девятого	сентября
10	Десятое	десятого	октября
11	Одиннадцатое	одиннадцатого	ноября
12	Двенадцатое	двенадцатого	декабря
13	Тринадцатое	тринадцатого	
14	Четырнадцатое	четырнадцатого	
15	Пятнадцатое	пятнадцатого	
16	Шестнадцатое	шестнадцатого	
17	Семнадцатое	семнадцатого	
18	Восемнадцатое	восемнадцатого	
19	Девятнадцатое	девятнадцатого	
20	Двадцатое	двадцатого	
21	двадцать первое	двадцать первого	
2...	двадцать ...	двадцать ...	
30	Тридцатое	тридцатого	
31	тридцать первое	тридцать первого	

Now let's sum everything up for different situations:

Listen to Track 58

Event + year/month (preposition в, prepositional case)

- **В каком году родился твой брат? В две тысячи двенадцатом.**
  When was your brother born? In 2012.

- **Когда у тебя отпуск? В августе.**
  When is your vacation? It's in August.

Event + month + year (preposition в, month–prepositional, year–genitive)

- **Когда ты начал работать в этой компании? В феврале две тысячи семнадцатого.**
  When did you start to work in this company? In February 2017.

Event + full date (all genitive)

- **Когда твои родители поженились? Двадцать пятого октября две тысячи шестого года.**
  When did your parents get married? On October 25, 2006.

Hey guys, this lesson was a little bit "mathy" and overloaded with grammar, but you are now 100% equipped for speaking about everything time-related in Russian. Don't forget to practice this new knowledge. It won't be hard as time surrounds us everywhere.

TIME TO PRACTICE!

Exercise 1 - Your friend asks you what time it is. Tell the time in the digital style. Try telling it in two ways: with the words "часов" and "минут" and without them. Don't forget to use the 12-hour time and specify the time of the day by adding the words "утра," "дня," "вечера," and "ночи."

1. 04:20 – четыре часа двадцать минут OR четыре двадцать утра
2. 06:00 – _____
3. 11:15 – _____
4. 13:00 – _____
5. 14:50 – _____
6. 16:00 – _____
7. 19:10 – _____
8. 23:40 – _____
9. 00:00 – _____
10. 01:15 – _____

Exercise 2 - Tell the time in the analogue style. Remember that Russians use the 12-hour time format for everyday communication. You can specify time using words "утра," "дня," "вечера," and "ночи."

1. 00:30 – полпервого ночи
2. 05:55 – _____
3. 06:15 – _____
4. 09:30 – _____
5. 12:10 – _____
6. 14:50 – _____
7. 18:25 – _____
8. 20:35 – _____
9. 22:45 – _____
10. 23:05 – _____

Exercise 3 - Translate the sentences into Russian:

1. My working day starts at 9:30.

   _____

2. I can't call Olga right now because it's already 2 a.m. in Moscow.

   _____

3. My friends and I usually meet in a cafe at noon to have lunch together.

   _____

4. Katya will come in the evening, at about eight o'clock.

   _____

Exercise 4 - Tell your friend what the date today is. Make sure you use the nominative case when telling the date in the abstract (without referring to an event):

1. February 3 –   Сегодня третье февраля.
2. March 10 –   _____
3. May 13 –   _____
4. June 20 –   _____
5. August 22 –   _____
6. October 25 –   _____
7. December 31 –   _____

Exercise 5 - Answer the questions in Russian following our example:

1. When will you come to Moscow? (August 23) – Двадцать третьего августа.
2. When do your summer holidays start? (June)

   _____

3. When were you born? (November 11, 2008)

   _____

4. When did you visit Russia last time? (September 2019)

   _____

Exercise 6 - Choose the right answer:

1. Двадцать минут четвертого.

   а) 4:20　　　б) 3:20　　　в) 18:20　　　г) 2:40

2. Полседьмого

   а) 6:50　　　б) 7:30　　　в) 16:30　　　г) 6:30

3. 10:27

   а) утро　　　б) день　　　в) вечер　　　г) ночь

4. 22:45

   а) без пятнадцати двенадцать

   б) без пятнадцати полночь

   в) без пятнадцати одиннадцать

   г) без пятнадцати двадцать два

5. Восемь тридцать два.

   а) 18:32　　　б) 8:33　　　в) 8:32　　　г) 20:32

Answers

Exercise 1

2. шесть (часов) утра, 3. одиннадцать пятнадцать утра, 4. час дня,
5. два пятьдесят, 6. четыре (часа) дня, 7. семь десять вечера, 8. одиннадцать сорок вечера, 9. двенадцать ночи OR полночь, 10. час пятнадцать ночи.

Exercise 2:

2. без пяти шесть, 3. четверть седьмого (утра), 4. полдесятого утра,
5. десять минут первого, 6. без десяти три, 7. двадцать пять минут седьмого,
8. без двадцати пяти семь, 9. без четверти одиннадцать,
10. пять минут двенадцатого.

Exercise 3

1. Мой рабочий день начинается в девять тридцать.
2. Я не могу позвонить Ольге сейчас, потому что в Москве уже два часа ночи.
3. Я обычно встречаюсь с друзьями в полдень, чтобы вместе пообедать.
4. Катя придет вечером около восьми.

Exercise 4

2. Сегодня десятое марта. 3. Сегодня тринадцатое мая. 4. Сегодня двадцатое июля. 5. Сегодня двадцать второе августа. 6. Сегодня двадцать пятое октября. 7. Сегодня тридцать первое декабря.

Exercise 5

2. В июне. 3. Одиннадцатого ноября две тысячи восьмого года. 4. В сентябре две тысячи девятнадцатого.

Exercise 6

1. б 2. г 3. а 4. в 5. Б

Lesson 6: Russian Nouns and Their Gender

Nouns are the first words we usually learn in a language. Naming people, things or ideas, they give us the first impression of a language. Also, nouns can predict the future. Wonder how? If nouns of a language you are going to learn have six grammatical cases, three genders, and two numbers, it means you are going to have some really crazy days ahead when your brain will boil. Just kidding. For Russian, it's not the case. After this lesson about Russian nouns and their gender, you will see that the Russian gender is very easy and doesn't cause any trouble at all.

What you should know about Russian nouns

Russian nouns mean a person, place, animal, thing, or an abstract idea (in fact, it's just what nouns in all languages do). At the same time, Russian nouns do have characteristics that make them special.

Unique features of Russian nouns

Russian nouns have:

Listen to Track 59

- **Three genders: masculine, feminine and neuter.**

  Gender is an inherent feature (not something a noun can change).

  For example, **дом** is always *masculine*, **кошка** is always *feminine*, and **молоко** is always *neuter*.

- **Two numbers (singular and plural).**

  Usually, nouns can change it, but some nouns are singular only (like **любовь**, **счастье**, **теннис**, **мебель** or **одежда**) and some are plural only (like **деньги**, **брюки**, **часы**, **ножницы** or **очки**).

- **Six cases (nominative, genitive, dative, accusative, instrumental, and prepositional).**

  Nouns can change cases depending on their role in a sentence. It is called declension.

All of these three features of Russian nouns are very important. And they should be learned in the above order, starting from the gender. You will see why.

Gender of Russian nouns

If you have ever had an experience in learning a language with gendered nouns (like French, for example), the word "gender" can make you cringe. Seems like someone who invented that language pranked us by deciding, "Let there be nouns of different genders that would require gender-specific articles before them, and let's make the division into genders absolutely illogical, hahaha!" Goodness, how else can we explain this absolutely irregular way the French divide their nouns into genders?

Good news! The Russian gender is a different cup of tea. It's 99% regular. No need to learn every noun's gender by heart. You only need to remember the endings every gender has, and using gendered nouns becomes a breeze. Of course, the exceptions exist, but they don't make trouble.

You probably won't realize how good this news is until you face this fact: in Russian, the gender rules all! It defines (directs and modifies) the flow of the language. And this is why.

Why is gender so determinative in Russian?

In Russian, gender is not only about nouns. It is also about adjectives, pronouns, numbers, participles, and even past tense verbs. All of these parts of speech decline by gender. The whole Russian language is gender-sensitive, which means if you master the Russian gender, you won't have issues with the rest of the language.

This is how it works. *thing, person, animal, a place*

Everything starts with a <u>noun</u>. For example, imagine we want to say something about spring (**весна**).

Listen to Track 60

Весна – *Spring*

Sounds good. Gender is already there because **весна** is feminine, but it's not so important as long as it is just one word. However, the very moment we decide to expand it and add some details, gender becomes determinative and starts to pop up from all parts of speech.

For example:

- <u>Ран**няя**</u> весна. – *Early spring. (adjective)*
- <u>Семнадцат**ая**</u> весна. – *Seventeenth spring. (number)*
- <u>Мо**я**</u> весна. – *My spring. (personal pronoun)*
- Весна <u>пришл**а**</u>. – *Spring came. (past tense verb)*

And finally, dragging it all in one sentence:

Пришл**а** мо**я** семнадцат**ая**, ранн**яя** весн**а**.– *My seventeenth, early spring has come.*

This sentence may sound a little bit artificial, but it is just an illustration of what real Russian is about. It is about gender. It means that to be able to speak Russian correctly, you need to know the gender of any noun you are talking about.

Whatever the sentence length, chances are that you will have to adjust words to the noun's gender at least once. That means you'll do it all the time.

Now that you fully realize how "VIP" Russian gender is, let's cut to the chase.

How to define gender in Russian

What do Russian genders mean?

1. When it comes to a person or an animal, the noun's gender usually (but not always) corresponds with the person's/animal's sex (male or female).

    Male → masculine noun gender.

    Female → feminine noun gender.

Listen to Track 61

For example:

- **мужчина** (*man, masculine*) — **женщина** (*woman, feminine*)
- **мальчик** (*boy, msc.*) — **девочка** (*girl, fem.*)
- **петух** (*cock, msc.*) — **курица** (*hen, fem.*)
- **кот** (*cat, msc.*) — **кошка** (*cat, fem.*)

2. Neuter nouns usually mean inanimate objects or abstract ideas. But still, there's a handful of neuter nouns that mean living beings:

Listen to Track 62

- **Дитя** – *child*
- **Божество** – *deity*
- **Существо** – *being, creature*
- **Ничтожество** – *nonentity, nobody*
- **Животное** – *animal* (sjvevotnoe)
- **Пресмыкающееся** – *reptile*
- **Млекопитающее** – *mammal*

3. When it comes to inanimate objects or ideas, they are usually masculine or feminine, and the gender is determined NOT BY THE NOUN'S MEANING, but by its ending.

How to define gender by endings in Russian

When we deal with objects, you need to know three simple rules to find out their gender.

When you look into your Russian dictionary, all nouns you find there are in their basic form—nominative case, singular (plural for plural-only nouns). This basic noun form has an ending, and this is how this ending defines the noun's gender:

Listen to Track 63

Gender	Endings	Example
Masculine	consonant or **-й**	Город (*city*), берег (*coast, shore*), мир (*world, peace*), дом (*house*), сад (*garden*), парк (*park*), год (*year*), месяц (*month*), март (*March*).
Feminine	**-а, -я**	Книга (*book*), квартира (*apartment*), работа (*work*), кастрюля (*pot*), земля (*ground, land*), семья (*family*).
Neuter	**-о, -е, -ё**	Дерево (*tree*), поле (*field*), окно (*window*), молоко (*milk*), бельё (*linen*), жилье (*accomodation*), остриё (*spike, edge*).

Most Russian nouns fit this simple scheme; however, exceptions still happen.

Nouns with irregular genders

Benefit one: there aren't many.

Benefit two: they are also quite regular.

Benefit three: they are easy to learn because every time you meet these nouns in a context (in a sentence with other words with gender-specific endings), this context teaches you about this noun's gender. Gendered nouns are absorbed naturally when you practice them in a context.

1. Nouns ending in **-ь** can be both masculine and feminine (but feminine are much more frequent). It is hard to explain why some are masculine and others are feminine. Just try to remember them:

Listen to Track 64

Masculine	Feminine
-ь	
Пут**ь** (*way*), кон**ь** (*horse*), нол**ь** (*zero*), июн**ь** (*June*), ден**ь** (*day*), пен**ь** (*stub*), etc.	Бол**ь** (*pain*), сол**ь** (*salt*), кров**ь** (*blood*), жизн**ь** (*life*), двер**ь** (*door*), ноч**ь** (*night*), мат**ь** (*mother*), доч**ь** (*daughter*), част**ь** (*part*), лен**ь** (*laziness*), etc.

2.   Masculine nouns meaning male persons ending in **-а, -я**:

Listen to Track 65

- Мужчин**а** – *man*
- Дяд**я** – *uncle or sometimes a male stranger*
- Дедушк**а** – *grandpa*
- Пап**а** – *dad, papa*
- Братишк**а** – *diminutive to a little brother, buddy*
- Парнишк**а** – *diminutive to a boy, lad*

3.   Neuter nouns ending in **-я**:

Listen to Track 66

- им**я** – *name*
- врем**я** – *time*
- брем**я** – *burden*
- плам**я** – *flame*

4.   Nouns of common gender (ending in **-а, -я**) can be both masculine and feminine, depending on the context:

Listen to Track 67

- сирот**а** – *orphan*
- коллег**а** – *colleague*

Here also belongs a set of nouns that denote a person with a remarkably strong characteristic, often negative:

- **обжора** – *glutton*
- **задира** – *bully*
- **транжира** – *spender*
- **соня** – *sleepyhead*
- **плакса** – *crybaby*
- **недотёпа** – *blunderer*

5. Nouns denoting professions are considered masculine, but if we talk about a female professional, the verb ending in the past tense will be female:

Listen to Track 68

- **секретарь** – *secretary, receptionist*
- **директор** – *managing director*
- **Наш контент-менеджер заболела.** – *Our content manager is sick.*

Adjectival gender endings

The gender of a noun impacts the gender of a related adjective. These are typical adjectival endings for masculine, feminine and neuter (in the nominative case):

Listen to Track 69

Masculine	Feminine	Neuter
-ий / -ый	-ая	-ое
Утром был сильн**ый** ливень. *It was raining very hard this morning.*	Моя старш**ая** сестра прожила в Англии пять лет. *My older sister has been living in England for five years.*	Море было тёпл**ое** и спокойн**ое**. *The sea was warm and calm.*

Gender of indeclinable nouns

Some Russian nouns don't decline by cases or numbers. It is because they are borrowed from foreign languages. Such nouns have non-typical endings for the Russian language, so we cannot rely on the endings to define the noun's gender. So how do we tell whether it's masculine, feminine or neuter? It's a case when the meaning helps a lot!

Listen to Track 70

Masculine	Feminine	Neuter	Masc. or fem. (depending on the context)
Animals/birds: • шимпанзе (*chimpanzee*) • пони (*pony*) • фламинго (*flamingo*) • кенгуру (*kangaroo*) **Male persons:** • месье (*monsieur*) • денди (*dandy*) • маэстро (*maestro*) **Occupations:** • конферансье (*master of ceremonies*) • атташе (*attaché*)	**Female persons:** • мисс (*miss*) • мадам (*madam*) • миссис (*missus*) • леди (*lady*) • фрау (*frau*) **Animals (if we know they are female):** • маленькая коала (*a small koala*) • огромная шимпанзе (*a huge chimpanzee*)	**Objects/items:** • пальто (*coat*) • меню (*menu*) • эскимо (*chocolate ice cream on a stick*) • пианино (*upright piano*) • алиби (*alibi*) • шоссе (*motorway*) • метро (*metro, subway*) • кино (*cinema*)	**Person:** • визави (*vis-à-vis, a person sitting in front of you*) • протеже (*protégé*)

Exceptions

The gender of some borrowed indeclinable nouns can be defined only by their direct meaning. They belong to the same gender as the words they can be replaced with (general words).

You should just memorize these exceptions:

Listen to Track 71

- **Пенальти** (*penalty*) is masculine because it can be replaced with **удар** (*kick*), which is masculine.
- **Кольраби** (*Hungarian turnip*) and **брокколи** (*broccoli*) are feminine because they can be replaced with **капуста** (*cabbage*), which is feminine.
- **Кофе** (*coffee*) and **латте** (*latte*) are masculine because they mean **напиток** (*drink*), which is masculine.
- **Салями** (*salami*) is feminine because **колбаса** (*sausage*) is feminine.
- **Авеню** *(avenue)* is feminine because **улица** (*street*) is feminine.

Gender of geographical names

Geographical terms accumulate toponyms from all over the world. Logically, their gender cannot be defined by their non-Russian endings. This is why we define their gender by their meaning (a general word).

For example:

Listen to Track 72

1. Names of cities, towns and islands are masculine because their general words **город** (*city*) or **остров** (*island*) are masculine:
   - Солнечн**ый** Маями– *sunny Miami*
   - Ярк**ий** Борнео – *bright Borneo*

2. *A lake* (озеро) is neuter:
   - Пресноводн**ое** Онтарио– *freshwater Ontario*

3. *A river* (река) is feminine:
   - Полноводн**ая** Миссисипи – *deep Mississippi*

4. *A country* (страна) is also feminine:
   - Жарк**ая** Конго – *hot Congo*

As you can see, the Russian way to define the gender of nouns is pretty regular, and where it is not regular, it's intuitive. The list of irregular gendered nouns is very short and easy to remember. Moreover, we have prepared a set of fun exercises to help you master Russian gendered nouns faster! Remember: when it comes to Russian gender, context is the best teacher. So never miss an opportunity to practice gendered nouns on real-life examples.

TIME TO PRACTICE!

Exercise 1 - Divide these nouns into three groups based on their gender:

Дождь, чувство, лень, мальчишка, жажда, боль, сочувствие, праздник, имя, профессор, климат, погода, зной, достижение, горе, август, телевидение, задание, речь, сочинение, забота, юность.

Masculine	Feminine	Neuter
дождь зной лень август боль речь праздник юность профессор климат	мальчишка жажда имя погода забота	чувство сочинение сочувствие достижение горе телевидение задание

Exercise 1.2—Complete the sentences choosing the correct adjective:

1. Это очень ... (трудный / трудная / трудное) часть текста.

   _____

2. Ты ... (самый лучший / самая лучшая / самое лучшее) в мире, братишка.

   _____

3. Оля — ... (маленький / маленькая / маленькое) сирота, она живет в детском доме.

   _____

4. Мой сосед по комнате — ... (страшный / страшная / страшное) соня, все время спит на диване.

   _____

5. (Исполнительный / исполнительная / исполнительное) директор захотела лично обсудить это с тобой.

   _____

6. Из-за коронавируса сейчас не ... (самый удачный / самая удачная / самое удачное) время для вечеринки.

   _____

Exercise 1.3—Complete the sentences with your own adjectives to describe the indeclinable nouns. Don't forget to put it in the noun's gender:

1. Тебе больше идет ... пальто.   – _____
2. На ветке сидел ... какаду.   – _____
3. Возле моего дома проходит ... шоссе.   – _____
4. В детстве у меня было ... пианино.   – _____
5. Присядь, я приготовлю тебе ... какао.   – _____
6. Когда в комнату вошла ... леди, все встали. – _____

Exercise 1.4—Divide these geographical names into three groups based on their gender:

Батуми, Тольятти, Лимпопо (river), Эри, Капри, Сомали, Бордо, Юнгфрау, Дели.

Masculine	Feminine	Neuter

Answers

Exercise 1

Masculine	Feminine	Neuter
Дождь, мальчишка, праздник, профессор, климат, зной, август.	Лень, жажда, боль, погода, речь, забота, юность.	Чувство, сочувствие, имя, достижение, горе, телевидение, задание, сочинение

Exercise 2

1. Трудная. 2. Самый лучший. 3. Маленькая. 4. Страшный. 5. Исполнительный. 6. Самое удачное.

Exercise 3

1. Серое. 2. Пёстрый. 3. Шумное. 4. Черное. 5. Теплое. 6. Элегантная.

Exercise 4

Masculine	Feminine	Neuter
Батуми (город), Тольятти (город), Капри (остров), Бордо (город), Дели (город).	Лимпопо (река), Сомали (страна), Юнгфрау (гора).	Эри (озеро).

Lesson 7: How to Create Plurals in Russian?

Cases, genders, and plurals are what makes Russian so special and enticing for language learners. (Let's admit it: if it's too easy, it doesn't turn us on).

We've tackled the gender issue in our previous lesson and proved that Russian genders aren't as unruly as someone might think. They turned out to be pretty regular.

As for the plurals, we won't lie to you and promise an easy win. Plurals are really an uphill journey you should brace yourself for and be patient. As your ultimate moral and mental support, we are here to help you out.

In this comprehensive guide on Russian plurals, we have collected everything you need to know to master the plural form.

A couple of important facts about Russian plurals

- Russian nouns have different forms according to three grammatical categories: gender, number and case.
- Russian nouns switch cases (decline) depending on their role in a sentence. Plural nouns do just the same. It means you should not only know the plural form of a noun but also how this plural form declines.
- The genitive form is very important because we use it with numerals when talking about quantities.

Sounds daunting, but don't worry. In the beginning, it is enough for you to learn the nominative, accusative and genitive forms. Other declension forms are much less frequent, and you can grasp them as you go along.

Before we get down to forming plurals, we need to put aside two groups of nouns that don't require plural forms. The first group is nouns that are used only in a singular form, and the second group is plural-only nouns (which are already in plural).

Single-only nouns in Russian

Listen to Track 73

- Uncountable substances such as **вода** (*water*), **молоко** (*milk*), **пиво** (*beer*), **масло** (*oil*), etc. (However, there can be plural forms when we mean "sorts" or "types".

  For example, **вина** (*wines, sorts of wine*).
- Abstract ideas such as **любовь** (*love*), **ненависть** (*hatred*), **счастье** (*happiness*) etc.
- Sports: **футбол** (*football*), **бокс** (*boxing*), **баскетбол** (*basketball*) etc.
- Collective nouns such as **обувь** (*shoes*), **мебель** (*furniture*), **белье** (*linen*), **посуда** (*dishware*) etc.

Plural-only nouns in Russian

Listen to Track 74

- **деньги** – *money*
- **ножницы** – *scissors*
- **брюки** – *trousers*
- **очки** – *glasses*
- **духи** – *perfume*
- **каникулы** – *holidays*
- **шахматы** – *chess*

For example:

- Вы не видели здесь мои **очки**? – *Have you seen my glasses here?*
- На нем были серые **брюки** и голубая рубашка. – *He was wearing grey trousers and a blue shirt.*

All other nouns create their plural forms using endings. This is how.

How to create plurals in Russian (nominative case)?

The nominative case is the basic case in Russian. It is used to denote a subject of a sentence.

The ending in the nominative case, plural depends on the noun's gender. This is how the endings change:

Listen to Track 75

Gender	Ending in sg → ending in pl.	Examples
Masculine	consonant → consonant + ы	студент (*student*) → студент**ы**
	-ь → и	корабль (*ship*) → корабл**и**
	-й → й	трамвай (*tram*) → трамва**и**
Feminine	-а → ы	звезда (*star*) → звёзд**ы**
	-я → и	семья (*family*) → семь**и**
	-ь → и	боль (*pain*) → бол**и**
	-ия → ии	авария (*accident*) → авар**ии**
Neuter	-о → а	озеро (*lake*) → озёр**а**
	-е → я	поле (*field*) → пол**я**
	-мя → ена	время (*time*) → врем**ена**
	-ие → ия	здание (*building*) → здан**ия**

Please note:

Feminine nouns ending in **-а** with stems ending in **г, к, х, ж, ч, ш, щ** in plural get the ending **-и** instead of **-ы.**

Listen to Track 76

For example:

- Нога → ног**и** (not ногы)
- Рука → рук**и** (not рукы)
- Лужа → луж**и** (not лужы)
- Свеча → свеч**и** (not свечы)
- Каша → каш**и** (not кашы)

Irregular plural forms

Some nouns create plural forms in a different way. They can be divided into six groups:

Listen to Track 77

Group	Example
Consonant → consonant + -**а** / -**я**	город (*city*) → город**а**
	доктор (*doctor*) → доктор**а**
	глаз (*eye*) → глаз**а**
	поезд (*train*)→ поезд**а**
	вечер (*evening*) → вечер**а**
	адрес (*address*) → адрес**а**
	паспорт (*passport*) → паспорт**а**
	слесарь (*locksmith*) → слесар**я**
Miscellaneous endings → -**ья**	брат (*brother*) → брат**ья**
	сын (*son*) → сынов**ья**
	друг (*friend*) → друз**ья**
	дерево (*tree*) → дерев**ья**
	крыло (*wing*) → крыл**ья**
	стул (*chair*) → стул**ья**
	лист (*leaf*)→ лист**ья**
	Note: please discern листья (*leaves*) and листы (*sheets*). They have a common singular form лист (*leaf, sheet*).
-**ец** (nationality) → -**цы**	испанец (*Spaniard*) → испан**цы**
	японец (*Japanese*)→ япон**цы**
	итальянец (*Italian*) → итальян**цы**
	британец (*British*) → британ**цы**
	американец (*American*)→ американ**цы**
-**нин** → -**не**	англичанин (*Englishman*) → англича**не**
	парижанин (*Parisian*) → парижа**не**
	гражданин (*citizen*) → гражда**не**
	христианин (*Christian*) → христиа**не**
	крестьянин (*peasant*) → крестья**не**

Absolutely irregular	ребёнок (*child*) → дети
	мать (*mother*) → матери
	дочь (*daughter*) → дочери
	яблоко (*apple*) → яблоки
	цветок (*flower*) → цветы
Single = plural	Here belong indeclinable nouns borrowed from foreign languages:
	кофе (*coffee*) → кофе
	какао (*cocoa*)→ какао
	пальто (*coat*) → пальто
	хобби (*hobby*) → хобби
	меню (*menu*) → меню

Declension of Russian plurals

We will have a look at two of the most frequently used cases—genitive and accusative.

Endings in the genitive case (plural)

The genitive case helps express relationship/possession and quantity when used with numbers.

The genitive form for plurals depends on the noun's type of declension:

(Please note that a "zero" ending in Russian means a missing ending. We mark it as an empty square.)

Listen to Track 78

1st declension type	2nd declension type	3rd declension type
Feminine, masculine nouns ending in **-а / -я** ↓ "zero" ending	Masculine nouns with "zero" (missing) endings + neuter nouns ending in **-о / -е** ↓ **-ов, -ев, -ей**	Feminine nouns with "zero" (missing) endings + nouns ending in **–ия** ↓ **-ей** (**-ий** for nouns ending in -ия)
женщина (*woman*) → женщин мужчина (*man*) → мужчин дедушка (*grandfather*) → дедушек работа (*job*) → работ страна (*country*) → стран	кот (*cat*) → кот**ов** стол (*table*) → стол**ов** гость (*guest*) → гост**ей** конь (*horse*) → кон**ей** море (*sea*) → мор**ей** брат (*brother*) → брать**ев**	ночь (*night*) → ноч**ей** мышь (*mouse*) → мыш**ей** история (*story*) → истор**ий**

The 2nd and the 3rd declension types are the most difficult for non-Russian speakers due to the many ending options. So here are a few tips for you:

Listen to Track 79

Gender	Ending in sg. → ending in pl. (genitive)	Examples
Masculine	-й, -ц → **-ев**	трамвай (*tram*) → трамва**ев** месяц (*month*) → месяц**ев**
	-ь → **-ей**	гость (*guest*) → гост**ей** конь (*horse*) → кон**ей** учитель (*teacher*) → учител**ей**
	all other masculine nouns → **-ов**	телевизор (*TV*)→ телевизор**ов** чайник (*kettle*)→ чайник**ов**
Feminine	-а → "zero" ending	квартира (*apartment*) → квартир
	-double consonant +а → "zero" ending (but an extra vowel – о, е – pops up to ease pronunciation)	девушка (*girl*) → девуш**е**к американка (*American woman*)→ американ**о**к чашка (*cup*) → чаш**е**к
	-consonant +я → **ь**	кастрюля (*pot*) → кастрюл**ь**
	-vowel +я → **й**	семья (*family*) → сем**ей** история (*story*) → истор**ий**
	-ь → **-ей**	боль (*pain*) → бол**ей**
Neuter	-о → "zero" ending (but an extra vowel may pop up to ease pronunciation)	окно (*window*) → ок**о**н озеро (*lake*) → озёр правило (*rule*) → правил
	-е → **-ей**	море (*sea*) → мор**ей** поле (*field*) → пол**ей**
	-ие → **-ий**	задание (*task*) → задан**ий**

How about the plural-only nouns we talked about earlier? Since we cannot find out their gender and singular form, we need to learn their plural genitive forms by heart:

Listen to Track 80

- часы (*watch, clock*) → час**ов**
- деньги (*money*) → денег
- ножницы (*scissors*) → ножниц
- брюки (*trousers*) → брюк
- очки (*glasses*) → очк**ов**
- духи (*perfume*) → дух**ов**
- каникулы (*holidays*) → каникул
- шахматы (*chess*) → шахмат

As you can notice, they have either "zero" endings or the endings **-ов**.

Endings in accusative case (plural)

We use the accusative case when we talk about direct objects.

Good news: this case doesn't have any specific endings. It just uses other cases' forms. For plural inanimate nouns, it takes the nominative's form, and for plural animate nouns, it borrows the genitive's form.

For example:

Listen to Track 81

- Я люблю своих родител**ей**. (Родитель, animate, nom. case, sg. → родител**ей**, gen. case, pl.) – *I love my parents.*
- Мой брат купил новые ботинк**и**. (Ботинок, inanimate, nom. case, sg. → ботинк**и**, nom. case, pl.) – *My brother bought new boots.*

How many: using plurals with numbers

Plural nouns often go with numbers (like "two dogs" or "three girls"). However, using numbers with nouns in Russian has one ~~pain~~ peculiarity. We need to put nouns into the genitive case. For English speakers, it will sound like "five of apples". Weird, but you'll get used to it.

Moreover, there are some other nuances that depend on the number itself (or rather its last digit).

Numbers ending in 1

For numbers ending in the word **один** (*one*), for example one (один), 31 (тридцать один), or 121 (сто двадцать один)—but not 11 (одиннадцать)—we use a noun in its singular form (its case will depend on the noun's role in a sentence). For example:

Listen to Track 82

- Одна тетрадь (sg., nom. case) – *one notebook*
- Один рубль (sg., nom. case) – *one rouble*
- Чай стоит шестьдесят один рубль (sg., accus. case) – *Tea costs sixty-one roubles.*

Numbers ending in 2, 3, 4

For numbers ending in the words **два** (*two*), **три** (*three*), or **четыре** (*four*), for example 24 (двадцать четыре), 103 (сто три) or 42 (сорок два), we use nouns in the genitive case, singular.

For example:

Listen to Track 83

- Две собаки – *two dogs*
- Три задания – *three tasks*
- Четыре доллара – *four dollars*
- Тридцать два сантиметра – *thirty-two centimetres*

Numbers ending in 5, 6, 7, 8, 9, 0, or -надцать

All the teens and numbers ending in the above digits require a noun in the genitive case, plural. This rule also refers to adverbs of quantity such as **много, мало**, etc.:

Listen to Track 84

- Одиннадцать (двенадцать, тринадцать... etc.) лет – *eleven (twelve, thirteen...) years.*
- Десять дней – *ten days*
- Двадцать минут – *twenty minutes*
- Тридцать шесть часов – *thirty-six hours*
- Много детей – *many children*

Please pay attention, that when it comes to age or a period of time that ends in the above numbers, a noun год (*year*) in the plural genitive will have an irregular form **лет**.

Compare:

Четыре **года** (*four years*), but пять **лет** (*five years*).

You'll get used to plurals and their genitive forms pretty fast if you practice them in context. You don't need to get into a special situation to be able to practice Russian plurals. Just count everything you see around. We also have a bundle of cool exercises to help you memorize plural forms faster.

TIME TO PRACTICE!

Exercise 1 - Put these nouns into the plural form where possible:

Свидание, дружба, путешествие, крикет, обувь, нож, комната, бутерброд, лист (of a tree), дерево, отвращение, игра, подруга, вечеринка, университет, ночь, приятель, буддист, ребенок, алиби, метро, француз, немец.

_____

_____

_____

Exercise 2 - Put the nouns in brackets into the genitive case to make them fit the context:

1. У меня с собой не было ... (деньги), и мой друг заплатил за меня.

   _____

2. На празднике было скучно без ... (сёстры).

   _____

3. Мы можем положить в пирог сливы вместо ... (яблоки).

   _____

4. У моих ... (друзья) есть домик на берегу озера.

   _____

5. С ... (деревья) падали желтые листья.

   _____

6. Дети хотели сделать для ... (учитель) сюрприз.

   _____

7. Я устал учиться, а до ... (каникулы) еще далеко.

   _____

Exercise 3 - Put these nouns into the accusative case, plural to make them fit the context:

1. Мы нашли в интернет-магазине отличные ... (термокружка).

   _____

2. Маша очень любит ... (ребенок).

   _____

3. По дороге на работу Миша встретил ... (приятель).

   _____

4. Я подарю тебе на день рождения ... (конфета).

   _____

Exercise 4 - Fill in the table using the numbers from the first column and nouns from the second column, making them plural. Follow our example:

Number	Noun, sg.	Number + noun, pl.
4	яблоко	Четыре яблока
25	день	
9	год	
120	страница	
360	градус	
24	час	
41	ребенок	
63	год	

Answers

Exercise 1

Свидание → свидания, дружба → (impossible), путешествие → путешествия, крикет → (impossible), обувь → (impossible), нож → ножи, комната → комнаты, бутерброд → бутерброды, лист → листья, дерево → деревья, отвращение → (impossible), игра → игры, подруга → подруги, вечеринка → вечеринки, университет → университеты, ночь → ночи, приятель → приятели, буддист → буддисты, ребенок → дети, алиби → алиби, метро → метро, француз → французы, немец → немцы.

Exercise 2

1. Денег. 2. Сестёр. 3. Яблок. 4. Друзей. 5. Деревьев. 6. Учителей. 7. Каникул.

Exercise 3

1. Термокружки. 2. Детей. 3. Приятелей. 4. Конфеты.

Exercise 4

Number	Noun, sg.	Number + noun, pl.
4	яблоко	Четыре яблока
25	день	Двадцать пять дней
9	год	Девять лет
120	страница	Сто двадцать страниц
360	градус	Триста шестьдесят градусов
24	час	Двадцать четыре часа
41	ребенок	Сорок один ребенок
83	год	Восемьдесят три года

Lesson 8: Russian Personal Pronouns

Pronouns are short words we use to replace nouns to make our conversation more vivid and less tautological. In Russian, there are so many pronouns and their forms (thanks to declension) that foreigners often get cold feet trying to wrap their heads around them. No worries! The trick here is to approach them gradually. First, get acquainted with personal pronouns and, after you are comfortable with them, move on to other types of pronouns. We promise to be around and help you out.

So, we start from the basics—personal pronouns and their declension.

Personal Pronouns in Russian

First of all, when do we need personal pronouns? You'll be surprised, but literally in every conversation. Personal pronouns help us mention a person or an object without naming them directly. We use them when we don't want to repeat the same nouns all the time.

Here are Russian personal pronouns and their English equivalents:

Listen to Track 85

Person	Singular	Plural
1st	**я** (*I*)	**мы** (*we*)
2nd	**ты** (*you*)	**вы** (*you*)
3rd	**он** (*he*) **она** (*she*) **оно** (*it*)	**они** (*they*)

At first glance, everything is like in English. Same division into persons, plural and singular. However, before you are off to use these pronouns in a conversation, you need to know a couple of things.

Firstly...

1. Perception of gender is different.

Listen to Track 86

In English, when we talk about an object (or an animal whose gender we don't want to emphasize), we use the pronoun **it**.

For example, a **cat** (кошка), a **TV** (телевизор), and a **window** (окно) can be referred to as **it**. In Russian, it's not that simple. The equivalent for **it** is **оно**, but we don't use it in the same way.

The point is that in Russian, every noun—be it animate or inanimate, a person or an animal—has an innate grammatical category of gender (masculine, feminine, or neuter). So you need to pick a pronoun based on a noun's gender: **кошка** will be referred to as **она**, **телевизор** as **он**, and **окно** as **оно**.

Please bear in mind that Russian gender as a grammatical category has nothing to do with biological sex (although it agrees with it). Objects like a pen (**ручка**, feminine) or a pencil (**карандаш**, masculine) also have genders even though they are inanimate.

You may think, "Hey, wait, you mean I need to know the gender of every noun to be able to use personal pronouns?"

Definitely! In Russian, gender is ubiquitous. You also need it for making nouns agree with adjectives and verbs, so we highly recommend learning new Russian nouns together with their gender.

And secondly...

2. All personal pronouns decline by cases.

To say a sweet phrase "I love you", you cannot just say "я люблю ты". You need to put **ты** in the accusative case: **я люблю тебя!** This table shows how to decline Russian personal pronouns. Sometimes declension changes not just the ending of a word, but the word entirely.

Declension of personal pronouns in Russian

Before you plunge into the table below, here are a few interesting facts that are going to make learning easier:

1. Genitive and accusative forms coincide.
2. Declension forms for **он** and **оно** coincide in all cases except the nominative case.

Listen to Track 87

Nominative case	я (I)	мы (we)	ты (you)	вы (you)	он (he)	она (she)	оно (it)	они (they)
Genitive case	меня	нас	тебя	вас	его	её	его	их
Dative case	мне	нам	тебе	вам	ему, **нему**	ей, **ней**	ему, **нему**	им, **ним**
Accusative case	меня	нас	тебя	вас	**его**	её, **неё**	**его**	их
Instrumental case	мной **(мною)**	нами	тобой **(тобою)**	вами	им, **ним**	ей **(ею)**, **ней (нею)**	им, **ним**	ими, **ними**
Prepositional case	мне	нас	тебе	вас	нём	ней	нём	них

This table can be hard to grasp for beginners, so we will follow up explaining the most difficult parts of it and providing examples.

Here are some keys to understanding:

Listen to Track 88

1. Pronounce **его** as "yeevoh".

2. Some pronouns when used after prepositions, get the first consonant sound **н** (this trick makes the language sound better):

    её — у **неё**

    ими — с **ними**

    ей — с **ней**.

For example:

- **Я её** целый день не видел. – *I haven't seen her all day.*
- У **неё** есть собака. – *She's got a dog.*
- Можешь пользоваться **ими** сколько хочешь. – *You can use them as long as you want.*
- Я поеду **с ними** на речку. – *I'll go to the river with them.*
- Возьми тряпку и вытри **ей** окно. – *Take the rag and wipe the window with it.*
- Моя сестрёнка очень веселая, **с ней** не соскучишься. – *My sister is very cheerful, she's never dull.*

3. Sometimes you can meet the extended forms of some pronouns: мной — **мною**, тобой — **тобою**, ей — **ею**, etc.

For example:

- Эта кисточка хорошая. **Ею** легко рисовать. – *This brush is good. It's easy to paint with it.*

And finally, a healthy portion of selfishness.

You already know what to call different persons and how to use pronouns to talk about objects. But the picture won't be full without a very special pronoun (also very personal and even a little bit selfish) we use to talk about actions we do to ourselves. This pronoun is called…

The personal reflexive pronoun "себя"

Listen to Track 89

It is the equivalent of English "self" we use to describe an action a person or an object does to themselves/itself (when the subject and the pronoun are the same person/object). And we've got good news for you because, unlike in English, where we have myself, yourself, himself, herself and other "selves", in Russian, there's only one reflexive pronoun — **себя**.

- Я люблю **себя**. – *I love myself. (Why not?)*
- Посмотри на **себя**! – *Look at yourself!*
- Мы слышим **себя**. – *We hear ourselves.*

As for the declension, it's very easy, and you need to memorize only three forms! **Себя** doesn't have a nominative case form because it never acts as a subject.

Listen to Track 90

Case	Себя	Examples
Nominative	---	---
Genitive	себя	Ты должен уметь постоять за **себя**. *You must be able to stand up for yourself.*
Dative	себе	Миша купил **себе** новую машину. *Misha bought himself a new car.*
Accusative	себя	Эта штора хорошо пропускает сквозь **себя** свет. *This curtain lets in enough light.*
Instrumental	собой (собою)	Ты, наверное, **собой** гордишься. *You must be proud of yourself.*
Prepositional	себе	Она немного рассказала о **себе**. *She told us a little bit about herself.*

Now you know how to use Russian pronouns and get up close and personal when needed. Don't forget to get a bit of practice because this topic requires lots of training. We've prepared a set of exercises on Russian personal pronouns for you to help you out with declensions.

TIME TO PRACTICE!

Exercise 1 - Replace the underlined words with a personal pronoun:

1. Я нашел <u>котенка</u> на улице. (acc. case)

   Я нашел его на улице.

2. <u>Окно</u> не закрывается. (nom. case)   – _____

3. Расскажи мне о <u>своей собаке</u>. (prep. case) – _____

4. <u>Тетради</u> нет в сумке. (gen. case)   – _____

5. На <u>столе</u> лежат книги. (prep. case)   – _____

6. Подойди ближе к <u>окну</u>, не бойся. (dat. case) – _____

Exercise 2 - Put the nouns in brackets into the correct case:

1. Почему (вы) не было на прошлом уроке? – _____

2. (Мы) собираемся в кино. Пойдешь с (мы)? – _____

3. Можно пригласить (ты) поужинать со (я) вместе? – _____

4. Давно (ты) дружишь с (она)? – _____

5. Я буду по (они) скучать. – _____

6. Вот чашка. Налей в (она) воды. – _____

Exercise 3 - Complete these phrases with any three persons at your discretion (you can use a reflexive pronoun as well). Follow our example:

Позвони... (мне, ей, им, etc.)

1. Одеть на ...   – _____

2. Любить ...   – _____

3. Все благодаря ...   – _____

4. Заглянуть внутрь ... – _____

5. Смеяться над ...   – _____

6. Убегать от ...   – _____

7. Приезжать к ...   – _____

8. Выглянуть из-за ... – _____

9. Благодарить ...   – _____

10. Пользоваться ...   – _____

Exercise 4 - Fill in the gaps with reflexive pronoun in the correct case:

1. После успешного выполнения задачи нужно похвалить...

   _____

2. Мой друг заказывает ... еду из ресторана.

   _____

3. Ты никогда ничего о ... не рассказываешь.

   _____

4. Он очень гордый и никого кроме ... не замечает.

   _____

5. Чтобы открыть дверь, нужно потянуть ее к ...

   _____

6. Сами по ... они отличные ребята.

   _____

Answers

Exercise 1

1. Я нашел его на улице. / 2. Оно не закрывается./ 3. Расскажи мне о ней./ 4. Ее нет в сумке. / 5. На нем лежат книги. / 6. Подойди ближе к нему, не бойся.

Exercise 2

1. Почему вас не было на прошлом уроке? / 2. Мы собираемся в кино. Пойдешь с нами? / 3. Можно пригласить тебя поужинать со мной вместе? / 4. Давно ты дружишь с ней? / 5. Я буду по ним скучать. / 6. Вот чашка. Налей в неё воды.

Exercise 3

1. Одеть на (себя, тебя, них). / 2. Любить (его, их, нас). / 3. Все благодаря (мне, тебе, нам). / 4. Заглянуть внутрь (него, меня, себя). / 5. Смеяться над (ними, ним, ней). / 6. Убегать от (нас, вас, них). / 7. Приезжать к (ним, вам, нам). / 8. Выглянуть из-за (него, них, тебя). / 9. Благодарить (себя, меня, тебя). / 10. Пользоваться (им, ею, ими).

Exercise 4

После успешного выполнения задачи нужно похвалить себя.

1. Мой друг заказывает себе еду из ресторана.
2. Ты никогда ничего о себе не рассказываешь.
3. Он очень гордый и никого кроме себя не замечает.
4. Чтобы открыть дверь, нужно потянуть ее к себе.
5. Сами по себе они отличные ребята.

Lesson 9: Russian Possessive Pronouns

Possessive pronouns come in handy when we talk about ownership (when something belongs to someone). They help replace a person's name or a possessive adjective, and thus, eliminate tautologies and make the language more flowing. Russian possessive pronouns aren't direct equivalents of English possessive pronouns. In this post, we will explain the difference and give you some great examples of how Russian pronouns can be used.

Russian possessive pronouns: important facts

Before we dig deeper into the topic, here are some few things you need to know about Russian possessive pronouns:

Listen to Track 91

1. Russian possessive pronouns **aren't equivalent to possessive pronouns in English**. They rather correspond to English possessive adjectives. For example:

мой → my

твой → your

его → his

2. Just like Russian adjectives, possessive pronouns are gender and number-sensitive. They also decline by cases. So you need to make them agree with the case, gender, and the number of a noun they modify.

For example:

- Мой город (город is masculine, singular) – *my city*
- Твоё изобретение (изобретение is neuter, singular) – *your invention*
- Наша работа (работа is feminine, singular) – *our work*
- Твои друзья (друзья is plural) – *your friends*

3. Please note that in Russian, we don't have an equivalent for English possessive pronouns such as *mine, yours, theirs* etc. Instead, to convey the same meaning, we use the word order.

Please, compare:

- Это **моя** книга. – *This is **my** book.*
- Эта книга **моя**. – *This book is **mine**.*

4. We use the reflexive possessive pronoun **свой** (one's own) when the owner is mentioned in the same sentence. We will talk more about it later in this lesson.

Possessive pronouns in Russian

Here's a list of Russian possessive pronouns together with their gender and number forms:

Listen to Track 92

English	masculine, sg	feminine, sg	neuter, sg	plural
My	мой	моя	моё	мои
Our	наш	наша	наше	наши
your	твой	твоя	твое	твои
your (pl.), Your	ваш, Ваш	ваша, Ваша	ваше, Ваше	ваши, Ваши
his	его	его	его	его
Her	её	её	её	её
Its	его	его	его	его
Their	их	их	их	их

As you can see, possessive pronouns **его** (*his*), **её** (*her*), **его** (*its*), and **их** (*their*) have easy-to-memorize fixed forms for all genders and numbers.

The "polite" possessive pronoun **Ваш** (*capital B*) is used in formal conversations when you want to sound more courteously.

Here are a few examples of how to use possessive pronouns in sentences:

Listen to Track 93

- **Мой** кот живет на нашей даче. – *My cat lives in our dacha.*
- Завтра приезжает **твоя** сестра. – *Tomorrow, your sister comes.*
- **Наше** решение лучше, чем ваше. – *Our solution is better than yours.*
- **Его** дети любят играть с нашими. – *His children like to play with ours.*
- **Её** книга стала мировым бестселлером. – *Her book became the world's bestseller.*
- **Их** любимое занятие — ездить верхом. – *Their favourite hobby is riding a horse.*
- С любовью, **ваша** дочь. – *With love, your daughter.*

By using possessive pronouns only in the nominative case (like in our examples), you can tell only about the subject (the subject is always in the nominative case). To be able to talk about objects and all kinds of subject-object relationships, you need to master the declension of possessive pronouns.

Declension of possessive pronouns

Listen to Track 94

Мой (my)

Case	masculine, sg	feminine, sg	neuter, sg	plural
Nominative	мой	Моя	моё	мои
Genitive	моего	моей	моего	моих
Dative	моему	моей	моему	моим
Accusative	мой (inanim.) моего (anim.)	мою	мое	мои (inanim.) моих (anim.)
Instrumental	моим	моей	моим	моими
Prepositional	моём	моей	моем	моих

Listen to Track 95

Наш (our)

Case	masculine, sg	feminine, sg	neuter, sg	plural
Nominative	наш	наша	наше	наши
Genitive	нашего	нашей	нашего	наших
Dative	нашему	нашей	нашему	нашим
Accusative	наш (inanim.) нашего (anim.)	нашу	наше	наши (inanim.) наших (anim.)
Instrumental	нашим	нашей	нашим	нашими
Prepositional	нашем	нашей	нашем	наших

Listen to Track 96

Твой (your)

Case	masculine, sg	feminine, sg	neuter, sg	plural
Nominative	твой	твоя	твоё	твои
Genitive	твоего	твоей	твоего	твоих
Dative	твоему	твоей	твоему	твоим
Accusative	твой (inanim.) твоего (anim.)	твою	твоё	твои (inanim.) твоих (anim.)
Instrumental	твоим	твоей	твоим	твоими
Prepositional	твоём	твоей	твоём	твоих

Listen to Track 97

Ваш (your/Your)

Case	masculine, sg	feminine, sg	neuter, sg	plural
Nominative	ваш	ваша	ваше	ваши
Genitive	вашего	вашей	вашего	ваших
Dative	вашему	вашей	вашему	вашим
Accusative	ваш (inanim.) вашего (anim.)	вашу	ваше	ваши (inanim.) ваших (anim.)
Instrumental	вашим	вашей	вашим	вашими
Prepositional	вашем	вашей	вашем	ваших

Listen to Track 98

Его, её, его, их (*his, her, its, their*)

You already know that possessive pronouns of the third person have fixed forms (**его**, **её**, **его**, **их**) that don't change by either gender or number. You can also use these same fixed forms for all cases.

For example:

- Я купил **его** маме цветы. (dative case) – *I bought flowers for her mom.*
- Мы нашли на столе **его** записную книгу. (accusative case) – *We found his notebook on the table.*
- **Её** машины не было возле дома. (genitive case) – *Her car wasn't near the house.*
- Я люблю сидеть у моря и наслаждаться **его** теплыми волнами. (instrumental case) – *I love sitting by the sea and enjoying its warm waves.*
- Об **их** смелости ходят легенды. (prepositional case)– *Their bravery is legendary.*
- Возле **их** дома есть автобусная остановка. (genitive case) – *There's a bus stop near their house.*

Please note: pronounce **его** as yee-voh and **её** as yee-yoh.

Reflexive possessive pronoun свой

In Russian, there is a special reflexive possessive pronoun **свой** (one's own). We use it instead of normal possessive pronouns when the subject and the owner are the same person.

Listen to Track 99

Please compare:

- Прочитай **свое** сочинение. – *Read **your** essay.*

and

- Прочитай сочинение. – *Read the essay.*

In the first sentence, the person we ask to read is the author (owner) of this essay. In the second sentence, the author (owner) is somebody else.

You may wonder why in Russian we cannot just use regular possessive pronouns **твой, мой, его, её** in all situations. Actually, there are lots of nuances here, which you may not understand at this level. So, until you get a real feel of the Russian language, we recommend sticking to the reflexive pronoun **свой** when the subject of a sentence and the owner coincide.

Listen to Track 100

More examples:

- Я ищу **свою** тетрадь (not Я ищу мою тетрадь). – *I am looking for **my** notebook.*
- Он любит **свою** жену (not Он любит его жену because it would sound like he loves someone else's wife). – *He loves his wife.*

The reflexive possessive pronoun **свой** agrees with a noun in gender, number, and case.

Declension of свой

Listen to Track 101

Case	masculine, sg	feminine, sg	neuter, sg	plural
Nominative	свой	своя	своё	свои
Genitive	своего	своей	своего	своих
Dative	своему	своей	своему	своим
Accusative	свой (inanim. своего (anim.)	свою	своё	свои (inanim. своих (anim.)
Instrumental	своим	своей	своим	своими
Prepositional	своём	своей	своём	своих

Listen to Track 102

For example:

- Я давно не видел **своего** друга. (gen. case) – *I haven't seen my friend for a long time.*
- Она не любит рассказывать о **своей** семье. (prep. case) – *She doesn't like telling about her family.*
- Ты допил **своё** молоко? (acc. case) – *Have you drunk your milk?*
- Покажи **своим** друзьям наш дом. (dat. case)– *Show our house to your friends.*

Congratulations! Now you know how to use all Russian possessive pronouns and even their reflexive form. The theory is good but practice is better. Declension is easier to grasp when you see it in real sentences. So feel free to check out the exercises we've prepared to help you out with possessive pronouns.

TIME TO PRACTICE!

Exercise 1 - Complete the sentences with appropriate forms of possessive pronouns. Pay attention to the gender, number, and case:

1. (Мой) ... другу исполнилось восемнадцать.   – _____
2. У (мой) ... сестры двое детей.   – _____
3. В (твой) ... доме очень много комнатных растений. – _____
4. Я мало что помню из (свой) ... детства.   – _____
5. По дороге мы встретили (твой) ... соседей.   – _____
6. Ты можешь пользоваться (мой) ... учебниками.   – _____
7. Сколько лет (твой) ... сестре?   – _____
8. Тебе нравится (твой) ... новое кресло?   – _____

Exercise 2 - Fill in the gaps with correct forms of possessive pronouns:

1. Я подписал открытку: "(Наш) ... дорогому папе".

   _____

2. Она не согласна с (их) ... новыми правилами.

   _____

3. (Ваш) ... новым заданием будет переписать текст.

   _____

4. Позвони (его) ... сестре и пригласи ее в гости.

   _____

5. Можно воспользоваться (ваш) ... уборной?

   _____

6. По-моему, это молоко несвежее, мне не нравится (его) ... вкус.

   _____

7. Начальник очень доволен (её) ... работой.

   _____

8. Расскажите нам о (ваш) ... планах.

   _____

Exercise 3 - The accusative case has two different forms for animate and inanimate nouns. Fill in the gaps with the correct possessive pronouns in the accusative case:

1. Соседка приходит каждый день, чтобы покормить (мой) ... котов.

   _____

2. Я принесу (ваш) ... заказ через минуту.

   _____

3. Ты не видел здесь (наш) ... Никиту?

   _____

4. Они быстро нашли (наш) ... дом.

   _____

5. Кто из (ваш) ... друзей умеет играть на гитаре?

   _____

6. Я давно не видел (твой) ... брата. Как он поживает?

   _____

7. Мы оценили (твой) ... старания в музыке.

   _____

8. Он посмотрел (мой) ... картины, и они ему очень понравились.

   _____

Exercise 4 - Complete the sentences by deciding whether a reflexive or a regular possessive pronoun is needed:

1. Идем, я познакомлю тебя со (моей/своей) мамой.

   _____

2. У него талант не замечать (его/свои) ошибки.

   _____

3. Я, кажется, потерял (твою/свою) книгу, прости.

   _____

4. Заканчивай делать (свое/его) домашнее задание и иди ужинать.

   _____

5. Мне нравится (твой/свой) район. Я бы тоже здесь жил.

   _____

6. Когда начинаются (твои/свои) каникулы?

   _____

Answers

Exercise 1

1. Моему / 2. Моей / 3. Твоем / 4. Своего / 5. Твоих / 6. Моими / 7. Твоей / 8. Твоё

Exercise 2

1. Нашему / 2. Их / 3. Вашим / 4. Его / 5. Вашей / 6. Его / 7. Её / 8. Ваших

Exercise 3

1. Моих / 2. Ваш / 3. Нашего / 4. Наш / 5. Ваших / 6. Твоего / 7. Твои / 8. Мои

Exercise 4

1. Своей. / 2. Свои / 3. Твою / 4. Свое / 5. Твой / 6. Твои

Lesson 10: An Easy Guide to Russian Adjectives

Gorgeous, long, orange, elegant, or *unimportant,* adjectives are responsible for describing people and objects. They are meant to add colours to our speech and make our language tastier. It's hard to imagine using a language without adjectives.... That is why in this guide, we are going to fill the gap and provide you with everything you need to know about Russian adjectives.

What you should know about Russian adjectives

– The role of adjectives in Russian is to describe nouns or pronouns.

For example:

Listen to Track 103

- **большое яблоко** *bolshoe yabloko* – *big apple*
- **деревянный стул** – *wooden chair*
- **красный диван** – *red sofa*

– An adjective normally precedes a noun in Russian. We use the inverted order to switch the focus over to an adjective.

– In Russian, the relationship between a noun and an adjective is very tender. Much more tender than in English, and this is why: an adjective is tied to a noun not only semantically, but also grammatically. An adjective adjusts to its noun, mimicking its grammar characteristics such as case, gender, and number. A noun declines, and so does its adjective(s). Later in this chapter, we will analyze how it happens.

– Your Russian dictionary lies to you. It gives only the initial form (nominative case, masculine gender, singular) and hushes up different forms for the other five cases, two genders, plural, and the short form. Foreigners often get cold feet when they get to this point.... But don't worry – in this guide, we've got you covered.

Three types of Russian adjectives

Listen to Track 104

Наташин (*Natasha's*), **большой** (*big*), and **апельсиновый** (*orange*) are three adjectives that can characterize a noun, for example, **торт** (*a cake*), but do it differently. Based on their connotation, all adjectives in Russian divide into three groups: qualitative, relative, and possessive.

1. Qualitative adjectives

When we need to describe the noun's characteristics that can be measured (such as weight, size, taste, temperature, color, speed, etc.), we use qualitative adjectives.

For example:

Listen to Track 105

глубокий (*deep*), **синий** (*blue*), **сладкий** (*sweet),* **вкусный** (*tasty*), **низкий** (*low*), **широкий** (*wide*), **огромный** (*huge*), **спокойный** (*calm*), **шумный** (*noisy*), etc.

If you can measure how much of a quality a noun has (for example, by adding the word "very" to an adjective), you are dealing with a qualitative adjective.

Such adjectives can create a short form and comparative form.

2. Relative adjective

Relative adjectives point to the fact that a noun has a relationship with another noun, which can mean several things, such as weight, length, time, location, action, material/source or purpose.

For example:

Listen to Track 106

- **вишнёвый торт** – *cherry cake* (**торт** is made from **вишня**)
- **детская одежда** – *children's clothes* (**одежда** is made for **дети**)
- **книжный магазин** – *bookstore* (**магазин** sells **книги**)
- **вчерашний фильм** – *yesterday's film* (**фильм** happened **вчера**)
- **итальянская кухня** – *Italian cuisine* (**кухня** originates from **Италия**) – location.

Relative adjectives create neither short forms nor comparative degrees.

3. Possessive adjectives

Possessive adjectives are a small group that explain whose this noun is. In English, we would create a possessive form from a noun by adding apostrophe + s. Russian has a system to turn nouns into possessive adjectives by using the suffixes **-ин, -ов (-ев), -ий, -овск (-евск)**, and **-инск (-ынск)**. Here's how it works:

Listen to Track 107

- **лиса** + **хвост** = **лисий хвост** – *fox's tail*
- **Маша** + **сумка** = **Машина сумка** – *Masha's bag*
- **отец** + **пример** = **отцовский пример** – *father's example*
- **мать** + **забота** = **материнская забота** – *mother's care*

Now you see why so many Russian surnames end with **-ов** or **-ев** (such as **Иванов**, **Петров**, **Алексеев**, **Васильев**, etc.). They historically were formed from possessive adjectives which denote that a person belongs to a certain family name.

Like relative adjectives, possessive adjectives also create neither short forms nor comparative degrees.

Declension of Russian adjectives (qualitative and relative)

An adjective in the Russian language is grammatically tied to a noun it modifies. This connection is so strong that an adjective adopts "its" noun's case, gender, and number.

So how do we decline adjectives in Russian?

The endings the adjective gets in every particular case depends on its own ending in the nominative (basic) case. There are three groups of adjectives depending on their stem ending.

1. Hard adjectives (ending in -ый, -ой)

Listen to Track 108

This group of adjectives is the biggest. This table shows how the endings change on two example adjectives: **белый** (*white*) and **простой** (*simple*). Please pay attention to the difference in the endings between animate (alive) and inanimate (not alive) adjectives.

	Masculine	Feminine	Neutral	Plural
Nominative	Бел**ый**	бел**ая**	бел**ое**	бел**ые**
Genitive	Бел**ого**	бел**ой**	бел**ого**	бел**ых**
Dative	Бел**ому**	бел**ой**	бел**ому**	бел**ым**
Accusative	бел**ый** (inanim.) бел**ого** (anim.)	бел**ую**	бел**ое**	бел**ые** (inanim.) бел**ых** (anim.)
Instrumental	Бел**ым**	бел**ой**	бел**ым**	бел**ыми**
Prepositional	о бел**ом**	о бел**ой**	о бел**ом**	о бел**ых**

Listen to Track 109

	Masculine	Feminine	Neutral	Plural
Nominative	Прост**ой**	прост**ая**	прост**ое**	прост**ые**
Genitive	Прост**ого**	прост**ой**	прост**ого**	прост**ых**
Dative	прост**ому**	прост**ой**	прост**ому**	прост**ым**
Accusative	прост**ой** (inanim.) прост**ого** (anim.)	прост**ую**	прост**ое**	прост**ые** (inanim.) прост**ых** (anim.)
Instrumental	Прост**ым**	прост**ой**	прост**ым**	прост**ыми**
Prepositional	о прост**ом**	о прост**ой**	о прост**ом**	о прост**ых**

2. Soft adjectives (ending in -ний)

Listen to Track 110

This small category of Russian adjectives always has a stressed stem. For example, **сИний** (*blue*) and **весЕнний** (*spring*).

	Masculine	**Feminine**	**Neutral**	**Plural**
Nominative	синий весенний	синяя весенняя	синее весеннее	синие весенние
Genitive	синего весеннего	синей весенней	синего весеннего	синих весенних
Dative	синему весеннему	синей весенней	синему весеннему	синим весенним
Accusative	синий (inanim.) синего (anim.) весенний (inanim.) весеннего (anim.)	синюю весеннюю	синее весеннее	синие (inanim.) синих (anim.) весенние (inanim.) весенних (anim.)
Instrumental	синим весенним	синей весенней	синим весенним	синими весенними
Prepositional	о синем о весеннем	о синей о весенней	о синем о весеннем	о синих о весенних

As you may have already noticed, Russian words are sometimes pronounced differently than the way they are written. The same is true here: the endings **-его**, **-ого** must be pronounced like [iva] and [ava]. For example: **синего** [*siniva*] and **белого** [*bielava*].

3. Adjectives with stems ending in к, г, х and ж, ш, ч, щ

Listen to Track 111

There are two groups of adjectives here depending on their endings in the basic form (masculine singular): **-ий** or **-ой**. Let's explain them using the examples of **маленький** (*small*), **плохой** (*bad*), and **большой** (*big*).

	Masculine	**Feminine**	**Neutral**	**Plural**
Nominative	маленьк**ий**	маленьк**ая**	маленьк**ое**	маленьк**ие**
Genitive	маленьк**ого**	маленьк**ой**	маленьк**ого**	маленьк**их**
Dative	маленьк**ому**	маленьк**ой**	маленьк**ому**	маленьк**им**
Accusative	маленьк**ий** (inanim.) маленьк**ого** (anim.)	маленьк**ую**	маленьк**ое**	маленьк**ие** (inanim.) маленьк**их** (anim.)
Instrumental	маленьк**им**	маленьк**ой**	маленьк**им**	маленьк**ими**
Prepositional	о маленьк**ом**	о маленьк**ой**	о маленьк**ом**	о маленьк**их**

The ending **-ой** is always stressed:

Listen to Track 112

	Masculine	**Feminine**	**Neutral**	**Plural**
Nominative	плох**ой** больш**ой**	плох**ая** больш**ая**	плох**ое** больш**ое**	плох**ие** больш**ие**
Genitive	плох**ого** больш**ого**	плох**ой** больш**ой**	плох**ого** больш**ого**	плох**их** больш**их**
Dative	плох**ому** больш**ому**	плох**ой** больш**ой**	плох**ому** больш**ому**	плох**им** больш**им**
Accusative	плох**ой** (inanim.) плох**ого** (anim.) больш**ой** (inanim.) больш**ого** (anim.)	плох**ую** больш**ую**	плох**ое** больш**ое**	плох**ие** (inanim.) плох**их** (anim.) больш**ие** (inanim.) больш**их** (anim.)
Instrumental	плох**им** больш**им**	плох**ой** больш**ой**	плох**им** больш**им**	плох**ими** больш**ими**
Prepositional	о плох**ом** о больш**ом**	о плох**ой** о больш**ой**	о плох**ом** о больш**ом**	о плох**их** о больш**их**

Declension of possessive Russian adjectives

Listen to Track 113

We will explain how to decline possessive adjectives using the example of **Катин** and **Алексеев**.

	Masculine	**Feminine**	**Neutral**	**Plural**
Nominative	Катин	Катин**а**	Катин**о**	Катин**ы**
Genitive	Катин**ого**	Катин**ой**	Катин**ого**	Катин**ых**
Dative	Катин**ому**	Катин**ой**	Катин**ому**	Катин**ым**
Accusative	**Катин** (inanim.) Катин**ого** (anim.)	Катин**у**	Катин**о**	Катин**ы** (inanim.) Катин**ых** (anim.)
Instrumental	Катин**ым**	Катин**ой**	Катин**ым**	Катин**ыми**
Prepositional	о Катин**ом**	о Катин**ой**	о Катин**ом**	о Катин**ых**

Listen to Track 114

	Masculine	**Feminine**	**Neutral**	**Plural**
Nominative	Алексеев	Алексеев**а**	Алексеев**о**	Алексеев**ы**
Genitive	Алексеев**а**	Алексеев**ой**	Алексеев**а**	Алексеев**ых**
Dative	Алексеев**у**	Алексеев**ой**	Алексеев**у**	Алексеев**ым**
Accusative	Алексеев (inanim.) Алексеев**а** (anim.)	Алексеев**у**	Алексеев**о**	Алексеев**ы** (inanim.) Алексеев**ых** (anim.)
Instrumental	Алексеев**ым**	Алексеев**ой**	Алексеев**ым**	Алексеев**ыми**
Prepositional	об Алексеев**ом**	об Алексеев**ой**	об Алексеев**ом**	об Алексеев**ых**

Short adjectives in Russian

In the very beginning we told you that, in Russian, adjectives are normally used before the nouns they modify. However, we can change this word order if we want to emphasize the adjective.

Listen to Track 115

For example:

- **Это высокое здание.** – *This is a high building.*
- **Это здание высокое.** – *This building is high.*

The inverted order is also associated with the use of a special form of Russian adjectives: short adjectives. We use them after nouns to make a statement. This is how we create short forms from complete adjectives in the example of **горячий** (*masculine*), **умная** (*feminine*), and **глубокое** (*neutral*):

- **Чай горяч.** – *The tea is hot.*
- **Она умна.** – *She is clever.*
- **Озеро глубоко.** – *The lake is deep.*

The good news is that you don't need to remember how to decline short adjectives since they are only used in the nominative case. The endings for short forms will be the following:

Complete	Masculine	Feminine	Neutral	Plural
красив**ый**	Красив	красив**а**	красив**о**	красив**ы**
глубок**ий**	Глубок	глубок**а**	глубок**о**	глубок**и**

Only qualitative adjectives can create short forms. For example, the adjectives **русский** (*Russian*) or **деревянный** (*wooden*), which are relative, doesn't have short forms.

Comparative degrees of Russian adjectives

At the beginning of this section, we mentioned that only qualitative adjectives denote qualities that can be measured, and therefore compared. They form the comparative and superlative degrees.

Comparative adjectives

When comparing one thing to another, we use a comparative degree. In Russian, you can do it in 3 easy ways.

Listen to Track 116

Using более (*more*), менее (*less*), and чем (*than*)

For example:

- **более удобный стул** – *a more comfortable chair*
- **менее интересная книга** – *a less interesting book*
- **Петр более эмоциональный, чем Дмитрий**. – *Peter is more emotional than Dmitriy.*

Creating comparative adjectives using suffixes -ee, -e, or -ше

Listen to Track 117

1. We add **-ee** if the stem ends in **н, л, р, п, б, м**, or **в**. For example:
   - трудный (*difficult*) – трудн**ee** (*more difficult*)
   - смелый (*brave*) – смел**ee** (*braver*)
   - быстрый (*fast*) – быстр**ee** (*faster*)
   - милый (*lovely*) – мил**ee** (*lovelier*)

2. Some stems get altered while creating a comparative degree. In this case, the ending **-e** is used:
   - лёгкий (*easy*) – легч**e** (*easier*)
   - дорогой (*expensive*) – дорож**e** (*more expensive*)
   - дешёвый (*cheap*) – дешевл**e** (*cheaper*)
   - большой (*big*) – больш**e** (*bigger*)

3. The suffix **-ше** helps create comparative forms for adjectives **старый** and **молодой**:
   - старый (*old*) – стар**ше** (*older*)
   - молодой (*young*) – млад**ше** (*younger*)

4. Some Russian adjectives have irregular comparative forms you should simply remember:
   - хороший (*good*) – лучше (*better*)
   - плохой (*bad*) – хуже (*worse*)
   - маленький (*small*) – меньше (*smaller*)

For example:

- **Я старше, чем мой брат.** – *I am older than my brother.*
- **Его машина дороже, чем моя.** – *His car is more expensive than mine.*

Listen to Track 118

Omitting чем (*than*)

In conversational Russian, we can create comparisons without the word **чем**. When doing it, we put the second noun into the genitive case and keep the word order fixed.

This is how it works:

- **Даша выше Нади.** – *Dasha is taller than Nadya.*
- **Его родители младше моих родителей.** – *His parents are younger than mine.*

Superlative adjectives

When we want to say that a noun has the highest or the lowest degree of some quality, we use superlative adjectives. There are two ways to create a superlative degree in Russian:

Listen to Track 119

1. Using suffixes **-ейш** or **-айш**:
   - красивый (*beautiful*) – красив**ейш**ий (*the most beautiful*)
   - великий (*great*) – велич**айш**ий (*the greatest*)

2. Sometimes we use another stem to create a superlative adjective:
   - **хороший** (*good*) – **лучший** (*the best*)
   - **плохой** (*bad*) – **худший** (*the worst*)

3. Using particles **самый**, **наиболее**, and **наименее**:
   - **самый умный студент** – *the cleverest student*
   - **самая красивая девушка** – *the most beautiful girl*
   - **наиболее выгодный вариант** –*the most winning option*

Please note that the particle **самый** declines as a regular hard adjective. The particles **наиболее** and **наименее** never change – we decline only the adjectives they go with.

Hooray, we've reached the bottom line! Of course, it's not the end of your Russian adjective journey, but we hope we've laid a good foundation for your future practice. The more you work with Russian adjectives, the more you notice they are not hard to remember.

TIME TO PRACTICE!

Exercise 1 - Put the adjectives in brackets into the correct form (gender, number, and case):

1. Мой папа купил (большой) арбуз. (*My dad bought a large watermelon.*)

   _____

2. Я расскажу об этом моей (лучший) подруге. (*I'll tell my best friend about it.*)

   _____

3. Я хорошо провел время со (старый) друзьями. (*I had a good time with old friends.*)

   _____

4. На столе лежат (новый) книги. (*There are new books on the table.*)

   _____

5. Я никогда раньше не видела такого (красивый) озера. (*I've never seen such a beautiful lake before.*)

   _____

6. Я люблю своего (старший) брата. (*I love my older brother.*)

   _____

7. Они приедут на (Сашин) автомобиле. (*They will arrive in Sasha's car.*)

   _____

Exercise 2 - Complete the sentences by underlining the correct adjectives and nouns. Please remember that animate and inanimate adjectives have different endings in the accusative case:

1. На улице мы встретили *белый кот* / *белого кота*. (*On the street we met a white cat.*)

2. Она одолжила *Светин шарф* / *Светиного шарфа*. (*She borrowed Sveta's scarf.*)

3. Мне легко запоминать *простые слова* / *простых слов*. (*It's easy for me to remember simple words.*)

4. На празднике я увидел *Машины знакомые* / *Машиных знакомых*. (*At the festival, I saw Masha's friends.*)

5. Макс принес мне *больших яблок* / *большие яблоки* для пирога. (*Max brought me big apples for a pie.*)

Exercise 3 - Create comparative adjectives following the examples:

1. Using suffixes **-ее**, **-е**, or **-ше**:

   Сильный – сильнее

   Близкий   – _____

   Далекий   – _____

   Красивый   – _____

2. Using **более**/**менее** and **чем**:

   Высокое здание – более высокое здание. – _____

   Крепкий кофе   – _____

   Сергей, талантливый, Михаил   – _____

   Овощи, полезный, чипсы   – _____

3. Without **чем**:

   Виктор, сильный, Владимир – Виктор сильнее Владимира.

   _____

   Моя сестра, старший, ты   – _____

   Питер, маленький, Москва   – _____

Exercise 4 - Fill in this table using all possible ways to create comparative and superlative adjectives:

Adjective	Comparative	Superlative
Умный (*clever*)	умнее, более умный	умнейший, самый умный, наиболее умный
Быстрый (*fast*)		
Популярный (*popular*)		
Привлекательный (*attractive*)		
Радостный (*happy*)		
Плохой (*bad*)		

Exercise 5 - Translate the sentences into Russian:

1. Pushkin is the most famous Russian writer.

   _____

2. Lakhta Center is the highest building in Russia.

   _____

3. Russia is the biggest country in the world.

   _____

4. The highest university in the world is located in Moscow.

   _____

5. Baikal is the deepest lake in Russia and the world.

   _____

Answers

Exercise 1

1. большой, 2. Лучшей, 3. Старыми, 4. новые, 5. красивого, 6. старшего, 7. Сашином.

Exercise 2

2. Светин шарф, 3. простые слова, 4. Машиных знакомых, 5. большие яблоки.

Exercise 3

1. ближе, дальше, красивее
2. более крепкий кофе, Сергей более талантливый чем Михаил, овощи более полезные чем чипсы
3. Виктор сильнее Владимира, моя сестра старше тебя, Питер меньше Москвы.

Exercise 4

Adjective	Comparative	Superlative
Умный	умнее, более умный	умнейший, самый умный, наиболее умный
Быстрый	быстрее, более быстрый	быстрейший, самый быстрый, наиболее быстрый
Любимый	более любимый	самый любимый
Привлекательный	привлекательнее, более привлекательный	самый привлекательный, наиболее привлекательный
Радостный	радостнее, более радостный	самый радостный, наиболее радостный
Плохой	Хуже	худший, самый плохой

Exercise 5

1. Пушкин – самый известный русский писатель. 2. Лахта Центр – самое высокое здание в России. 3. Россия – самая большая страна в мире.
4. Самый высокий университет мира находится в Москве.
5. Байкал – самое глубокое озеро в России и в мире.

Lesson 11: Tenses in Russian—Part 1: Infinitives and Present Tense

Life has three "tenses" – past, present, and future – and so does the Russian language. This is hard to digest for those who have 15 or 18 tenses in their native language. Seems like Russians approach tenses philosophically and don't complicate life (which is already complicated enough) with tangled grammar. In this chapter we will take a look at Russian tenses and their forms (there are some), so join us – it's going to be fun and easy.

Why does Russian have only three tenses?

If you google the issue, you'll find lots of conflicting points of view. Some (non-Russian-speakers mostly) will tell you that Russian has at least 18 tenses (two infinitives, two perfective indicatives, three imperfective indicatives, two conditionals, three participles, two gerunds, two passive participles, and two imperatives). They compare Russian with something they already know (English or French) and try to find similarities.

Others, mostly Russians, will insist **there are only three tenses** because ... they know it from school!

Why is there such a huge gap between the two theories? And why do Russians see only three tenses where the non-Russian world sees 18?

- Modern Russian philologists specializing in morphology don't treat aspects (perfective and imperfective) as tenses but rather as a separate grammar category. Aspects don't create tenses in Russian.
- Perfective and imperfective verbs are different verbs in Russian, not forms of the same verb.
- Unlike in English, some forms of Russian verbs are treated as moods (indicative, subjunctive, and imperative) or participles rather than tenses.

For these simple reasons, modern Russian has only 3 tenses:

1. **Present tense** (of imperfective verbs)
2. **Past tense** (of imperfective and perfective verbs)
3. **Future compound** (of imperfective verbs) **and future simple** (of perfective verbs)

Before we move on to these 3 tenses, we have to start from the basics – the basic form of a verb called the infinitive.

Infinitive verbs

What is an infinitive in Russian?

Listen to Track 120

The infinitive is the verb form you meet in your dictionary. Apart from the action description, the Russian dictionary provides information about the verb's aspect (perfective or imperfective). Accordingly, the infinitive verb answers two different questions: **Что делать?** and **Что сделать?** In English, these two questions sound the same way: *What to do?* However, in Russian they are two different questions:

- **Что делать?**: **смотреть** (*to look*), **слушать** (*to listen*), **идти** (*to go*), **читать** (*to read*), **спать** (*to sleep*), **учить** (*to learn*), **любить** (*to love*), **строить** (*to build*) (imperfective, action is in process)
- **Что сделать?**: **посмотреть** (*to look*), **послушать** (*to listen*), **пойти** (*to go*), **прочитать** (*to read*), **поспать** (*to sleep*), **выучить** (*to learn*), **полюбить** (*to love*), **построить** (*to build*) (perfective, action is complete)

These questions prove the statement we mentioned above: in Russian, perfective and imperfective verbs are different verbs, not forms of the same verb. You see, **делать** (*to do*) and **сделать** (*to do*) are different verbs in Russian.

Russian infinitives have a wide range of endings (such as **-ать, -ять, -уть, -еть, -оть, -ыть, -чь, -ти, -ить, -зть, -сть**) which can be hard to remember. For a start, you need to remember at least these most common ones: **-чь, -ти,** and **-ть**.

Infinitive verbs are not used that often in a sentence because, in Russian, verbs have to be altered according to their gender, case, number, and of course tense, depending on their role in the sentence. Nevertheless, there are at least six situations when we need an infinitive.

When do we use infinitives in Russian?

Listen to Track 121

1. To form the compound future tense:
   - **Я буду делать** домашнее задание. – *I **will do** my homework.*
   - Татьяна **будет играть** на гитаре, а я **буду петь**. – *Tatyana **will play** the guitar, and I **will sing**.*

2. With verbs meaning beginning, ending, or continuation of an action.

- **Я начинаю учить** русский язык. – *I **start to learn** Russian.*

- Они **продолжат строить** новую школу. – *They **will keep building** a new school.*

- Никита **закончил писать** свое сочинение. – *Nikita **finished writing** his essay.*

3. After the words **должен** (*must*), **готов** (*ready*), **рад** (*glad*), **намерен** (*intend*), and **обязан** (*obliged*):

- Я **должен прочитать** эту книгу до понедельника. – *I **must read** this book by Monday.*

- Вы **готовы потратить** на это такие деньги? – *Are you **ready to pay** that much for it?*

- Мы будем **рады увидеться** снова. – *We will be **glad to see** you again.*

- Я **намерен доказать,** что они ошибаются. – *I **intend to prove** they are wrong.*

- Он **обязан заботиться** о семье. – *He is **obliged to take care** of his family.*

4. With predicative adjectives and adverbs such as **трудно** (*difficult*), **надо/нужно** (*should, have to, need*), **можно** (*it is possible, may*), **необходимо** (*necessary, need*), and **нельзя** (*shouldn't, can't*):

- Мне **трудно понять**, о чем этот текст. – *It is **difficult** for me **to understand** what this text is about.*

- **Надо мыть** руки перед едой. – *You **should wash** your hands before the meal.*

- **Можно поговорить** с твоей сестрой? – ***May I talk** to your sister?*

- Вам **необходимо заполнить** анкету. – *You **need to fill** out a form.*

- Мне **нельзя есть** шоколад, у меня аллергия. – *I **shouldn't eat** chocolate; I'm allergic to it.*

5. With some verbs of motion (**идти, ехать, лететь, ходить**, etc.):

- Я **иду** в магазин **купить** свежий хлеб. – *I **am going** to the shop **to buy** fresh bread.*

- Моя сестра **летит** в Россию **изучать** русский язык. – *My sister **is going** to fly to Russia to study Russian.*

6. When infinitive acts as a subject:

- Рано **вставать** --- хорошая привычка. – ***Getting up*** *early is a good habit.*

You see, nothing is difficult about the infinitive in Russian. The next time you read a Russian text, pay attention to infinitives and think about which one of the six "infinitive situations" it is.

So we move on to the first of the three tenses, the easiest one.

Present tense (настоящее время)

Present tense in the Russian language describes actions happening in the present, including those happening in the moment of speaking. Thus, the Russian present tense is a pretty versatile way to speak about actions, whereas English-speakers need three tenses – present simple, present continuous, and present perfect continuous.

For example:

Listen to Track 122

- **Я живу в России** (present tense). – *I live in Russia.* (present simple)
- **Я учу русский язык** (present tense). – *I am studying Russian.* (present continuous)
- **Я живу в России всю жизнь** (present tense). – *I have been living in Russia for my whole life.* (present perfect continuous)

We aren't going to say that there are no other ways to translate those English phrases into Russian. There are. We just wanted to show how versatile Russian is and how much depends on the context.

The present tense is really simple, and we promise you'll soon become a present tense ninja, but first you need to master a true sacral mystery of the Russian Language, which is…

Two conjugation types of Russian verbs

Conjugation means the way a verb changes form for each person. There are two conjugation types of verbs in Russian, and they have to do with the infinitive endings. If you have been paying attention, those endings are **-ать, -ять, -уть, -еть, -оть, -ыть, -чь, -ти, -ить, -зть, -сть**. Now, look at how they are classified by conjugation types.

1. First conjugation type

Listen to Track 123

All Russian verbs with endings -**ать**, -**ять**, -**оть**, -**уть**, -**еть**, -**ть** belong here. To conjugate them, you need to remove -**ть** and add an appropriate ending according to the person. Let's take the verbs **читать** (*read*) and **писать** (*write*) as examples:

- Я чита**ю**. – *I read.*
- Ты чита**ешь**. – *You read.*
- Он/она/оно чита**ет**. – *He/she/it reads.*
- Мы чита**ем**. – *We read.*
- Вы чита**ете**. – *You read.*
- Они чита**ют**. – *They read.*
- Я пиш**у**. – *I write.*
- Ты пиш**ешь**. – *You write.*
- Он/она/оно пиш**ет**. – *He/she/it writes.*
- Мы пиш**ем**. – *We write.*
- Вы пиш**ете**. – *You write.*
- Они пиш**ут**. – *They write.*

Eleven verbs are exceptions to this rule: **дышать** (*to breathe*), **держать** (*to keep*), **гнать** (*to drive*), **слышать** (*to hear*), **ненавидеть** (*to hate*), **смотреть** (*to look*), **вертеть** (*to twirl*), **терпеть** (*to endure*), **видеть** (*to see*), **обидеть** (*to offend*), and **зависеть** (*to depend*).

2. Second conjugation type

Listen to Track 124

These are the verbs with endings **-ить**, **-еть** and those 11 irregular verbs from the paragraph above. To conjugate them, just remove **-ить/-еть** and add an appropriate ending according to the person. This is how they conjugate (using the examples of **дышать** and **учить**):

- Я дыш**у**. – *I breathe.*
- Ты дыш**ишь**. – *You breathe.*
- Он/она/оно дыш**ит**. – *He/she/it breathes.*
- Мы дыш**им**. – *We breathe.*
- Вы дыш**ите**. – *You breathe.*
- Они дыш**ат**. – *They breathe.*
- Я уч**у**. – *I study.*
- Ты уч**ишь**. – *You study.*
- Он/она/оно уч**ит**. – *He/she/it studies.*
- Мы уч**им**. – *We study.*
- Вы уч**ите**. – *You study.*
- Они уч**ат**. – *They study.*

Almost done! There is one important **note** for you before you go.

Foreigners find it hard to understand where to write endings -у(т) or -а(т) and -ю(т) or -я(т). There is a simple spelling rule about it: after the letters **ш, щ, ж, ч, ц, к, г,** and **х,** write **у** and **а** and never **ю** or **я**. Example:

Listen to Track 125

- **Я дышу** (*I breathe*) not дышю.
- **Я учу** (*I learn*) not учю.
- **Они дышат** (*They breathe*) not дышят.
- **Они учат** (*They learn*) not учят.

That's everything you need to know about Russian infinitives and the present tense. Make sure you take time to practice conjugation with the most popular Russian verbs. We recommend you to learn them with their conjugation type until you grasp the principle and it becomes fluent.

TIME TO PRACTICE!

Exercise 1 - Find the odd one out:

1. Бродить лезть кататься класть беру стоять покидать – _____

2. Писать мочь схватить убрать убраться котится – _____

3. Рисовать рассказать прочесть посмотрит пить дать – _____

4. Играть вернуть отойти отойди заснуть спать – _____

Exercise 2 - Correct the sentences putting the verbs in brackets into the infinitive form:

1. Сегодня я буду (готовлю) мое любимое блюдо. (*Today I will cook my favorite dish.*)

   _____

2. Мой брат только начинает (работает) учителем в школе. (*My brother is just starting to work as a school teacher.*)

   _____

3. Продолжай (учи) язык, и у тебя все получится. (*Keep learning the language, and you will succeed.*)

   _____

4. Когда закончишь (делаешь) домашнее задание, мы пойдем гулять. (*When you finish your homework, we'll go for a walk.*)

   _____

5. Он должен (написал) сочинение до среды. (*He must write an essay by Wednesday.*)

   _____

6. Если тебе трудно (запомнит) новые слова, надо (записывал) их в блокнот. (*If you find it difficult to remember new words, you should write them down in a notebook.*)

   _____

Exercise 3 - Write down the given verbs into two columns according to their conjugation type:

Ходить, видеть, лежать, иметь, слышать, обидеть, молчать, держать, колоть, дышать, лить, кушать, гнать, любить, терпеть, путешествовать, катать, читать

First conjugation type	Second conjugation type

Exercise 4 - Put the verbs in brackets into the correct form:

1. Ты (любить) мороженое? (*Do you like ice cream?*)

   _____

2. Мы с сестрой (бывать) в Москве каждый год. (*My sister and I visit Moscow every year.*)

   _____

3. Сегодня мой друг (играть) в футбол, и я (идти) его поддержать. (*Today my friend is playing football, and I am going to support him.*)

   _____

4. Моя коллега и я вместе (бегать) по утрам. (*My colleague and I run together in the morning.*)

   _____

5. Обычно я (начинать) свое утро с чашки горячего кофе. (*I usually start my morning with a cup of hot coffee.*)

   _____

6. Наш пес (дышать) так громко, что мы (слышать) его с другой комнаты. (*Our dog breathes so loudly that we can hear him from the other room.*)

   _____

7. Мне нужно (носить) очки, потому что я плохо (видеть). (*I need to wear glasses because I can't see well.*)

   _____

Answers

Exercise 1

1. беру, 2. котится, 3. посмотрит, 4. отойди.

Exercise 2:

1. готовить, 2. работать, 3. учить, 4. делать, 5. написать,
6. запомнить, записывать.

Exercise 3

First conjugation type	Second conjugation type
Лежать	ходить
Иметь	видеть
Молчать	слышать
Колоть	обидеть
Лить	держать
Кушать	дышать
Путешествовать	Гнать
Катать	любить
Читать	терпеть

Exercise 4

1. любишь, 2. бываем, 3. играет, иду, 4. бегаем, 5. начинаю,
6. дышит, слышим, 7. носить, вижу.

Lesson 12: Tenses in Russian—Part 2: Past Tense

Russian language has only three tenses: present, past, and future. Today, we are talking about the past tense, which enables you to tell stories and describe all past events, completed or not. One tense for all types of past actions. Sounds good, doesn't it? Join us in this lesson and get ready to tell your story. Let's go!

Past "simple"? No, past "the only"!

So, how did it happen that English has past simple, past continuous, past perfect, and past perfect continuous, but Russian has only one past tense? The point is that Russian has the concept of aspects – a grammatical feature that tells whether the action is completed or not.

- **Perfective aspect** means that the action is completed.
- **Imperfective aspect** means incomplete, repeated, reversed, ongoing, or habitual actions.

Hence Russian doesn't need four separate past tenses for different types of past actions because it has two types of verbs – perfective and imperfective. It will be easier to understand if you look at this example:

Listen to Track 126

Past simple	*I **read** a book about Russia yesterday.*	Я вчера **читал** книгу о России.
Past continuous	*I **was reading** a book last night.*	Я **читал** книгу вчера вечером.
Past perfect	*I knew how to do it. I **had read** a book about it before.*	Я знал, как это сделать. Я про**читал** книгу об этом раньше.
Past perfect continuous	*My eyes hurt. I **had been reading** five hours straight.*	Мои глаза болели. Я **читал** пять часов подряд.

As you can see, all four situations are translated into Russian using the same past tense, but two verbs are imperfective (**читал**) and two are perfective (**про, читал**). We remind you again that in Russian, perfective and imperfective verbs are different verbs (**читал** and **прочитал**), not forms of the same verb.

Present perfect is the past tense in Russian

Here goes another brain twister for English speakers. The present perfect tense doesn't have an equivalent in the Russian language. It is because, from the Russians' point of view, the action cannot be completed in the present. If it is completed, it is in the past. That is why all present perfect phrases are translated into Russian using the regular past tense but that of perfective verbs.

Listen to Track 127

- Я **прочитала** три книги о России. – *I **have read** three books about Russia.*
- Иван **прожил** в России всю свою жизнь. – *Ivan **has lived** in Russia for his whole life.*
- Я не голоден. Я **съел** бутерброд и **выпил** чаю. – *I'm not hungry. I **have eaten** a sandwich and **have drunk** some tea.*

Прочитать, прожить, съесть and **выпить** are perfective verbs as opposed to **читать, жить, есть** and **пить**, which are imperfective.

Remember: everything that has been done (regardless of how you understand the time when it has been done) needs the Russian past tense of the perfective verb to describe it. The same goes for the present perfect continuous as well:

- Я устал. Я **проработал** за компьютером весь день. – *I am tired. I **have been working** on my computer for the whole day.*

Negative statements in the past tense

1. If you want to tell about the action that never happened, use the imperfective verb in the past tense:

Listen to Track 128

- Я **не смотрела** телевизор вчера вечером. – *I **didn't watch** TV last night.*
- Мы **не хотели** вас беспокоить. – *We **didn't want** to disturb you.*
- Мой друг Майк никогда **не жил** в России. – *My friend Mike **has never lived** in Russia.*
- Мы **не видели** друг друга десять лет. – *We **haven't seen** each other for ten years.*

Note that the last two phrases are translated with the present perfect tense although, in Russian, imperfective verbs are used. Why? The point is in the action duration. If the action is prolonged in time (including "never" statements), Russians use imperfective verbs.

2. If the action failed to happen despite the intention, use the perfective verb in the past tense:

Listen to Track 129

- Я **не смог** прийти вчера. – *I **failed to come*** *yesterday.*
- Он **не позвонил**. – *He **hasn't called*** *me.*
- Маша **не сделала** домашнее задание. – *Masha **hasn't done*** *her homework.*
- Я **не понял** это предложение. – *I **didn't understand*** *this sentence.*

Questions in the past tense

Listen to Track 130

1. When you are interested whether the action was completed successfully, use the perfective verb:
   - Ты **купила** угощение к празднику? – ***Have*** *you **bought*** *the holiday treats?*
   - Вы уже **посмотрели** новый фильм Марвел? – ***Have*** *you **watched*** *the new Marvel movie yet?*

2. In all other cases, use the imperfective verb:
   - Кто **читал** новую книгу Пратчетта? – *Who **read** the new book by Pratchett?*
   - Ты **бегал** сегодня утром? – *Did you **jog** this morning?*

If you are not sure which verb to use – perfective or imperfective – try to convert the question into a statement and see what fits best.

And now we are getting to the most exciting part!

How to form the past tense in Russian

Russian doesn't have any auxiliary verbs for creating the past tense. It is formed by altering the verb itself.

Note: Russian infinitives have three types of endings: **-ть**, **-ти**, and **-чь**. Accordingly, there are three types of past tense formation.

Past tense of infinitives ending with -ть

Listen to Track 131

Let's create the past tense of the verbs **петь** (*sing*), **смотреть** (*watch*), **играть** (*play*), and **читать** (*read*).

1. Remove the ending **-ть**.
2. Add an ending according to the gender:
   - **-л** (masculine)
   - **-ла** (feminine)
   - **-ло** (neutral)
   - **-ли** (plural)

Я	пел, пела	смотрел, смотрела	играл, играла	читал, читала
Ты	пел, пела	смотрел, смотрела	играл, играла	читал, читала
Он	пел	смотрел	играл	Читал
Она	пела	смотрела	играла	Читала
Оно	пело	смотрело	играло	Читало
мы, вы, они	пели	смотрели	играли	Читали

Listen to Track 132

Please, pay attention that **я** (*I*) and **ты** (*you*) also have genders in the Russian language, so adjust the endings according to the subject's gender, for example:

- я делал – *I did (I am a man)*
- я делала – *I did (I am a woman)*
- ты делал – *You did (you are a man)*
- ты делала – *You did (you are a woman)*

Past tense of infinitives ending with -ти

Listen to Track 133

Let's create past tense of the verbs **нести** (*carry*), **везти** (*carry, convey*), and **трясти** (*shake*).

1. For the masculine, remove the ending **-ти**.
2. Otherwise, add:
   - **-ла** (feminine)
   - **-ло** (neutral)
   - **-ли** (plural)

Я	нёс, несла	вёз, везла	тряс, трясла
Ты	нёс, несла	вёз, везла	тряс, трясла
Он	нёс	Вёз	Тряс
Она	несла	Везла	Трясла
Оно	несло	Везло	Трясло
мы, вы, они	несли	Везли	Трясли

If you have noticed, in masculine form the Russian letter "**е**" in the stem gets replaced with "**ё**" ([jo] as in "Yo, dude!").

Listen to Track 134

This type of past tense formation has one crucial exception you need to know right away. It is the verb **идти** (*to go*). It forms the past tense in a pretty weird way. Just learn it without trying to understand (no one does):

Я	шёл, шла
Ты	шёл, шла
Он	шёл
Она	шла
Оно	шло
мы, вы, они	шли

Past tense of infinitives ending with -чь

Listen to Track 135

Let's create the past tense of the verbs **печь** (*bake*), **беречь** (*spare, take care of*), and **течь** (*flow*).

1. For the masculine, replace **-чь** with **-к** (after soft vowels **я, ё, ю, и, е**) or **-г**.
2. For feminine, neutral, and plural, add these endings to the masculine ending:
   - **-ла** (feminine)
   - **-ло** (neutral)
   - **-ли** (plural)

Я	пёк, пекла	берёг, берегла	тёк, текла
Ты	пёк, пекла	берёг, берегла	тёк, текла
Он	Пёк	берёг	тёк
Она	пекла	берегла	текла
Оно	пекло	берегло	текло
мы, вы, они	пекли	берегли	текли

Past tense of reflexive verbs

Listen to Track 136

In Russian, there is such thing as reflexive verbs, which we use when the subject and the object of the sentence are the same person. Such verbs simply mean doing something to oneself and have the endings **-ся** and **-сь**.

For example:

лечить**ся** (*receive treatment*), купать**ся** (*take a bath*), старать**ся** (*do one's best*), печь**ся** (*bake oneself*), or трясти**сь** (*tremble, shiver*).

You have probably noticed that before the endings **-ся** or **-сь**, these verbs normally have infinitive endings **-ть, -ти,** or **-чь**, which we already know about (and know how to put them in the past tense).

Reflexive verbs create the past tense in the same way as non-reflexive infinitives do but keep their reflexive ending (**-ся** or **-сь**).

For example:

Я	лечился, лечилась	купался, купалась	старался, старалась	пёкся, пеклась	трясся, тряслась
Ты	лечился, лечилась	купался, купалась	старался, старалась	пёкся, пеклась	трясся, тряслась
Он	Лечился	купался	старался	пёкся	Трясся
Она	Лечилась	купалась	старалась	пеклась	Тряслась
Оно	Лечилось	купалось	старалось	пеклось	Тряслось
мы, вы, они	Лечились	купались	старались	пеклись	Тряслись

Wow, that was huge! We hope you had fun with Russian grammar and learned how to "age" Russian verbs by making them past. Now it's time for you to practice. Try to form the past tense for the following verbs and memorize them:

Listen to Track 137

Быть (*to be*), **мочь** (*can*), **уметь** (*to be able to*), **иметь** (*to have*), **жить** (*to live*), **хотеть** (*to want*), **видеть** (*to see*), **слышать** (*to hear*), **любить** (*to love*), **знать** (*to know*), **понять** (*to realize*), **ходить** (*to walk*), **спасти** (*to save*), **давать** (*to give*), **дать** (*to give*), **спать** (*to sleep*) etc.

TIME TO PRACTICE!

Exercise 1 - Translate the sentences into Russian paying attention to the verb aspect (perfective or imperfective):

1. Yesterday I watched a new movie about pirates.

_____

2. My dad has been working in a bank for 10 years.

_____

3. I used to play basketball when I was a child.

_____

4. My sister and I have visited Saint Petersburg twice.

_____

Exercise 2 - Fill in the table forming the past tense for the given verbs. Keep in mind that for я and ты, Russian verbs have both masculine and feminine forms:

	спать	ползти	жить	мочь	звонить	радоваться	Учиться
Я	спал, спала						
Ты	спал, спала						
Он							
Она							
Оно							
мы, вы, они							

Exercise 3 - Put the verbs in brackets into the past tense:

1. Мы (идти) по дорожке в парке и (увидеть) ежа. (*We were walking along a path in the park and saw a hedgehog.*)

   _____

2. Из пекарни (доноситься) приятный аромат, там (печься) булочки с корицей. (*A pleasant aroma wafted from the bakery, where cinnamon rolls were baked.*)

   _____

3. Матвей (стараться) сдать тест на отлично и поэтому (учиться) всю ночь. (*Matvey tried to pass the test perfectly and therefore studied all night.*)

   _____

4. Когда я (приехать) в Москву, я совсем не (знать) русского языка. (*When I arrived in Moscow, I didn't know Russian at all.*)

   _____

Exercise 4 - Rewrite the sentences transforming the present tense into the past tense:

На улице солнечная погода. На небе нет ни одной тучки. Однако я все равно беру с собой зонт, потому что к вечеру обещают дождь. После работы мы с друзьями идем на футбол.

_____

_____

_____

_____

Answers

Exercise 1

1. Вчера я смотрел новый фильм про пиратов. 2. Мой отец проработал в банке десять лет. 3. Я играл в баскетбол, когда был маленьким. 4. Я и моя сестра были в Санкт-Петербурге дважды.

Exercise 2:

	спать	ползти	жить	мочь	звонить	радоваться	Учиться
Я	спал, спала	полз, ползла	жил, жила	мог, могла	звонил, звонила	радовался, радовалась	учился, училась
Ты	спал, спала	полз, ползла	жил, жила	мог, могла	звонил, звонила	радовался, радовалась	учился, училась
Он	спал	полз	жил	мог	звонил	радовался	Учился
Она	спала	ползла	жила	могла	звонила	радовалась	Училась
Оно	спало	ползло	жило	могло	звонило	радовалось	Училось
мы, вы, они	спали	ползли	жили	могли	звонили	радовались	Учились

Exercise 3

1. шли, увидели, 2. доносился, пеклись, 3. старался, учился, 4. приехал, знал.

Exercise 4

На улице была солнечная погода. На небе не было ни одной тучки. Однако я все равно взял с собой зонт, потому что к вечеру обещали дождь. После работы мы с друзьями пошли на футбол.

Lesson 13: Tenses in Russian—Part 3: Future Tense

Time flies! We have already told you about the present and past tenses in Russian, and today, it's time for the third and last one — the future tense. After this lesson, you will be able to talk about your plans, describe upcoming events and — who knows? — maybe even foretell the future! Ready? Let's start.

What is the future tense for?

As you may have noticed, Russians take grammatical time (or tense) literally. We mentioned that the present tense refers only to incomplete actions taking place in the present and never refers to accomplished actions. If the action is complete, it is no longer in the present. It is in the past (tense). All ongoing, habitual, or simply incomplete actions that took place in the past also require the past tense.

According to this simple time logic, the future tense is used for ALL actions that are going to take place after the moment of speaking, whether they are complete or incomplete actions. The Russian future tense has two forms: simple and compound.

Future simple tense

The future simple is also called perfective because it is for the <u>perfective verbs only</u>. The future simple is formed using personal endings (conjugation):

Listen to Track 138

- Я до**ем** завтрак и потом провер**ю** почту. – *I **will finish** my breakfast and then I **will check** my email.*
- Он прочита**ет** сообщение вечером и скаж**ет**, что он думает. – *He **will read** the message tonight and **tell** us what he thinks.*
- Прид**ет** весна, и дни стан**ут** дольше. – *The spring **will come**, and days **will become** longer.*

We already know about the conjugation of Russian verbs from the present tense chapter. Here, it works in the same way but with one difference: in the present tense, all verbs were imperfective, but here verbs are perfective. In other words, they mean an accomplished action.

Listen to Track 139

For example, in the present tense, we say **я ем** (*I eat*). This is the imperfective verb, and its infinitive form is **есть**. We cannot form the future simple tense using the verb **есть**. We need its perfective counterpart, i.e. **съесть** or **доесть**. We take one of these verbs and form the future simple form:

- Я **съем** бутерброд, когда проголодаюсь. – *I will eat a sandwich when I get hungry.*

We have mentioned already that, in Russian, <u>perfective and imperfective verbs are different verbs, not forms of the same verb</u>. Very often the perfective verb is formed based on the imperfective verb using prefixes:

Listen to Track 140

- **делать** (*do*) – **сделать**
- **читать** (*read*) – **прочитать**
- **писать** (*write*) – **написать, выписать, записать, дописать**
- **пить** (*drink*) – **выпить, отпить**
- **звонить** (*call*) – **позвонить**
- **ехать** (*go, ride, drive*) – **приехать, заехать, проехать, выехать, наехать**

As perfective and imperfective verbs have the same endings, their conjugation is also the same (please read the chapter about the present tense in Russian where we described two types of conjugation).

When do we use the future simple tense?

Listen to Track 141

1. Action will be completed or the emphasis is on its result:
   - Я **позвоню** тебе завтра утром. – *I **will call** you tomorrow morning.*
   - Маша **приготовит** на ужин лазанью. – *Masha **is going to cook** lasagna for dinner.*
   - Я **допишу** статью к обеду. – *I **will have written** the article by noon.*

2. A single, brief action in the future:
   - Миша **забежит** поговорить вечером. – *Misha **will drop by** to talk tonight.*
   - На выходных я **поеду** к родителям. – *This weekend, I am **going to go** to my parents.*
   - Костя **поужинает** с друзьями сегодня. – *Kostya **will dine** with his friends tonight.*

3. Action that is going to take place immediately after the moment of speaking (sometimes even merging with the present):
   - Я **перезвоню** вам через несколько минут. – *I'll **call** you **back** in a few minutes.*
   - Мы сейчас **повернем** налево и **увидим** большую площадь. – *We **will** now **turn** left and **see** a big square.*

4. Expressing a wish, instruction, or a command:
   - **Позвонишь** мне, когда доберешься домой. – ***Call** me when you get home.*
   - **Скажешь** ему, чтобы помыл посуду. – ***Tell** him to wash the dishes.*

5. In Russian proverbs:
   - Что **посеешь**, то и **пожнешь**. – *You **reap** what you **sow**.*

6. Negative statements with an absent subject (2nd person singular):
   - Сюжет такой запутанный, ничего **не поймешь**. – *The plot is so tangled that one can't understand a thing.*
   - Ничего **не поделаешь**. – *Nothing can be done (OR: It can't be helped).*

The future simple is also often used in narratives instead of the past tense. You will probably meet a lot of it when you read Russian literature.

In this chapter, we focus instead on the uses of the future simple tense in casual Russian. And now we move on to another way to form the future tense.

Future compound tense

Listen to Track 142

The future compound tense is also called imperfective because it is formed using the conjugated verb "to be" (**быть**) and infinitive:

> **быть** + **infinitive**

Look at how we create the future compound tense for the verb **читать** and pay attention to how the verb **быть** is conjugated:

- Я буд**у читать** книгу. – *I will read a book.*
- Ты буд**ешь читать** книгу. – *You will read a book.*
- Он (она/оно) буд**ет читать** книгу. – *He (she/it) will read a book.*
- Мы буд**ем читать** книгу. – *We will read a book.*
- Вы буд**ете читать** книгу. – *You will read a book.*
- Они буд**ут читать** книгу. – *They will read a book.*

Yup, this is much easier than the simple future tense where you have to keep in mind the conjugation type of each verb. Here, you need to get only one verb (**быть**) conjugated and add any suitable verb from the dictionary (infinitive form) to speak about future events.

When do we use the future compound tense?

Listen to Track 143

1. Action that will be in the progress in the future:
   - Я **буду читать** книгу еще час. – *I **will be reading** a book for one more hour.*

   The focus is on the process, not completion.

   - Мы **будем стараться** закончить проект вовремя. – *We **will do** our best to finish the project on time.*

   The focus is not on finishing the project, but on the effort (process).

2. Future action as a fact without consideration of its result:
   - Завтра мы **будем писать** контрольную работу. – *We **will take** a test tomorrow.*

   We just name the action that will take place in the future — the result isn't important.

   - Мы **будем учить** глагол после имени существительного. – *We **will study** the verb after the noun.*

   We focus neither on the result nor on the process. We just point to the fact.

3. Repeated actions in the future:

- **Буду повторять тебе** снова и снова, пока ты наконец не поймешь. *I **will keep repeating** it to you again and again until you finally understand.*
- Во время лечения он **будет принимать** это лекарство дважды в день. *During the therapy, he **will take** this medicine twice a day.*

Now that you know the uses of both future simple and future compound tenses in Russian, practice a little bit. Imagine a situation in the future, decide which type of use it is and create some phrases. The language is best learned if you apply it to real-life situations.

Although the mission seems to be complete, it isn't. Hold on, just one important thing before you go…

When English present becomes Russian future…

As you know, English has the "zero" conditional plus three other conditional forms that describe different levels of possibility for the situation you are talking about. Let's look at the zero and first conditional, as they are linked with the Russian future tense more than you think.

- *If you freeze water, it becomes ice.*

What we see is the classic example of <u>zero conditional</u> that describes a general truth. However, where English uses the present simple tense in the main clause, Russians are more prone to use the future simple:

Listen to Track 144

- Если заморозить воду, она **превратится** в лед.

  OR

- Если вы **заморозите** воду, она **превратится** в лед.

As you can see, the future simple tense can also be used in the if-clause in Russian. This doesn't mean you can't use the present tense for telling general truths in Russian (although it sounds a little bit ~~weird~~ uncommon). We just warn you that Russians see it in a slightly different way.

The first conditional in Russian is also more "future" than it is in English. Just compare the English phrases and their Russian equivalents:

Listen to Track 145

- Если **пойдет** дождь, мы **не пойдем** гулять. – *If it rains, we will not go for a walk.*

- Если **позвонишь** Маше, она **расскажет** тебе о проекте. – *If you call Masha, she will tell you about the project.*

In Russian, we use the future simple tense <u>in both the if-clause and the main clause.</u> It's kind of a strict rule. Maybe this is explained by the fact that the present tense in Russian has only imperfective verbs which cannot express the idea of a condition taking place. That is why a perfective verb is required here.

Congratulations! Our journey across the Russian tense system is over. Now you can speak about all kinds of events that ever happen. We hope that Russian tenses weren't hard to understand.

TIME TO PRACTICE!

Exercise 1 - Conjugate the verbs in brackets to create future simple tense. Follow the example:

1. Я (дочитать) эту книгу сегодня и (отдать) тебе. → Я дочитаю эту книгу сегодня и отдам тебе. (*l will finish this book today and give it to you.*)

2. Папа (доесть) свой завтрак и (отвезти) тебя в школу. (*Dad will finish his breakfast and drive you to school.*)

   _____

3. Учитель (зайти) в класс, и урок (начаться). (*The teacher will enter the classroom and the lesson will begin.*)

   _____

4. Мы (позвонить) тебе вечером и (сказать) наше решение. (*We will call you in the evening and tell you our decision.*)

   _____

5. Миша (купить) к ужину вина и (приготовить) салат. (*Misha will buy wine for dinner and prepare a salad.*)

   _____

Exercise 2 - Put the verbs in brackets into the compound future tense. Memorize how the verb to be (быть) is conjugated:

1. На совещании мой босс (быть, рассказывать) об успехах нашей компании. (*At the meeting, my boss will talk about the success of our company.*)

   _____

2. Ты (быть, отвечать) на мой вопрос? (*Will you answer my question?*)

   _____

3. Мои друзья не (быть, брать) с собой в путешествие палатку, поэтому ее (быть, брать) я. (*My friends will not take a tent with them on the trip, so I will take it.*)

   _____

4. Сегодня вы (быть, рисовать) пейзаж, потому что наш урок рисования (быть, проходить) на природе. (*Today you will draw a landscape, because our drawing lesson will take place outdoors.*)

   _____

Exercise 3 - Rewrite the sentences transforming the future compound tense into the future simple tense. Notice how perfective verbs change the meaning of a sentence:

1. Маша будет готовить для нас вечером свой любимый коктейль. → Маша приготовит для нас вечером свой любимый коктейль. (*Masha will prepare her favorite cocktail for us in the evening.*)

   _____

2. Сегодня я буду ужинать у своего друга. (*Today I will have dinner at my friend's house.*)

   _____

3. Они будут стараться закончить уборку до обеда. (*They will try to finish cleaning before lunch.*)

   _____

4. После завтрака отец будет работать в саду. (*After breakfast, my father will work in the garden.*)

   _____

Exercise 4 - Conjugate the verbs in the future simple tense:

	Позвонить	съесть	Выпить	Пойти	Дать	узнать	Поиграть
Я							
ты							
он, она, оно							
Мы							
Вы							
они							

Answers

Exercise 1

2. доест, отвезет, 3. зайдет, начнётся, 4. позвоним, скажем, 5. купит, приготовит.

Exercise 2:

1. будет рассказывать, 2. будешь отвечать, 3. не будут брать, буду брать, 4. будете рисовать, будет проходить.

Exercise 3

2. Поужинаю, 3. постараются, 4. поработает.

Exercise 4

	Позвонить	съесть	выпить	пойти	дать	узнать	Поиграть
Я	Позвоню	съем	выпью	пойду	дам	узнаю	Поиграю
ты	Позвонишь	съешь	выпьешь	Пойдешь	дашь	узнаешь	поиграешь
он, она, оно	Позвонит	съест	выпьет	пойдет	даст	узнает	Поиграет
Мы	Позвоним	съедим	выпьем	пойдем	дадим	узнаем	Поиграем
Вы	Позвоните	съедите	выпьете	пойдете	дадите	узнаете	поиграете
они	Позвонят	съедят	выпьют	пойдут	дадут	узнают	поиграют

Lesson 14: Russian Verbs of Motion

In English, you can describe different kinds of motion using the same versatile verb "to go," whether they: (1) happen in the moment of speaking, (2) happen regularly, or (3) refer to the use of transportation.

In Russian, we've got separate verbs for all types of motion. That is why foreigners easily get confused when dealing with these verbs. We are here to help you get this tangled topic straight.

What's the difference between English and Russian verbs of motion?

In English, we learn the exact meaning of a motion verb from the context. In Russian, motions verbs are pretty self-explanatory. One verb means a specific type of motion and nothing else. From this point of view, the Russian motion verb system is easier to understand (even though the effect is spoiled by the conjugation, haha).

For example:

- *I am **going** to the gym.*
- *I usually **go** to the gym on Mondays, Wednesdays, and Fridays.*
- *I usually **go** to the gym by bus, but today I am **going** to the gym by car.*

In Russian, we don't have one versatile verb that would fit all of these situations. Instead, we have **four** unique verbs for each particular context:

Listen to Track 146

- Я **иду** в спортзал. (*I **am going** to the gym.*)
- Я обычно **хожу** в спортзал по понедельникам, средам и пятницам. (*I usually **go** to the gym on Mondays, Wednesdays, and Fridays.*)
- Я обычно **езжу** в спортзал на автобусе, но сегодня я **еду** на машине. (*I usually **go** to the gym by bus, but today I am **going** to the gym by car.*)

Here is how these four verbs are conjugated:

Listen to Track 147

Person	идти	ходить	ехать	ездить
Я	иду	Хожу	еду	Езжу
Мы	идём	Ходим	едем	Ездим
Ты	идёшь	Ходишь	едешь	ездишь
Вы	идёте	Ходите	едете	Ездите
он, она, оно	идёт	Ходит	едет	Ездит
Они	идут	Ходят	едут	Ездят

These verbs may seem overwhelming, but there's nothing to worry about. If you practice regularly, you'll grasp them soon and will speak like a pro. Keep reading, and we will explain how to choose the right verb and sound like a native speaker.

This choice is mainly dictated by these three verb characteristics:

- Direction of movement
- Perfective/Imperfective aspect
- Method of movement

Direction of movement: where are we going?

Listen to Track 148

Previously we talked about four verbs of motion (**идти, ходить, ехать, ездить**) that differ in their meaning and usage. They are actually not four separate verbs, but two pairs of the verbs of motion: **идти/ходить** (*go on foot*), and **ехать/ездить** (*go by car*). We will look at 15 more pairs of verbs of motion later in this chapter.

Each pair has two forms of the verb depending on its directionality:

- Unidirectional
- Multidirectional

(The first verb in a pair is unidirectional, the second one is multidirectional, respectively.)

Listen to Track 149

Unidirectional verbs of motion such as **идти** or **ехать** mean a single movement (even though it can be prolonged in time) that happens only in one direction.

For example:

- Я сейчас **иду** на работу. – *I am **going** to work now.*
- Ты **идешь** сегодня вечером на вечеринку? – *Are you going to the party tonight?*
- Мария **едет** в Москву встретиться с друзьями. – *Maria is **going** to Moscow to see her friends.*

All three examples explain movements that occur only once and only in one direction. It is not necessary that these movements happen in the moment of speaking. Nonetheless, if you see adverbs **now** or **today**, it means that the context requires a unidirectional verb of motion.

Listen to Track 150

Multidirectional verbs of motion such as **ходить** and **ездить** mean movement in multiple directions, habitual or repeated movements, or movements as abilities.

For example:

- Мой брат совсем маленький, он даже еще не умеет **ходить**. – *My brother is very young; he can't even **walk** yet.*
- Я **хожу** на баскетбол по средам. – *I **go** to play basketball on Wednesdays.*

Adverbs of frequency such as **обычно** (*usually*), **часто** (*often*), **иногда** (*sometimes*), **всегда** (*always*), **каждое воскресенье** (*every Sunday*), etc. help indicate that we need to use a multidirectional verb of motion.

Aspect: perfective or imperfective?

If you have read our previous chapters about Russian tenses, you must have already learned that Russian verbs can be perfective or imperfective. Only unidirectional verbs of motion can have both perfective and imperfective aspects. However, perfective verbs can be used only in the past and future tenses. The present tense is for imperfective verbs only.

Listen to Track 151

For example, the verbs **идти** and **ехать** are unidirectional, and they are imperfective. They don't have a perfective counterpart in the present tense, but the past and future tense do have them:

	Imperfective	**Perfective**
Present	Она **идет** домой. *She's going home.* Она **едет** домой на метро. *She's going home by subway.*	-------------------------------------
Past	Она **шла** домой. *She was going home.* Она **ехала** домой на метро. *She was going home by subway.*	Она **пошла** домой. *She's gone home.* Она **поехала** домой на метро. *She's gone home by subway.*
Future	Она **будет идти** домой. *She will be going home.* Она **будет ехать** домой на метро. *She will be going home by subway.*	Она **пойдет** домой. *She will go home.* Она **поедет** домой на метро. *She will go home by subway.*

As you can see, the perfective verbs of motion are created with the use of the prefix **по-** (**пошла/ пойдет**, **поехала/поедет**). They have an inchoative meaning, i.e. they mark the beginning of an action.

By contrast, imperfective verbs of motion describe repeatable or ongoing actions where the focus is on the process rather than beginning or completeness.

Method: how is the action performed?

Listen to Track 152

The method of movement — whether you go by foot or by transport — will define your choice of the motion verb. As you may have already noticed, the verbs **идти** and **ходить** mean to go by foot (or when the way we get to a place isn't important) while **ехать** and **ездить** mean to go somewhere using transportation.

All transport expressions in Russian require the preposition **на** followed by the noun (mode of transport) in the prepositional case.

For example:

- **ехать на машине** – *go by car*
- **ехать на автобусе** – *go by bus*
- **ехать на метро** – *go by subway*
- **ехать на такси** – *go by taxi, take a cab*
- **ехать на трамвае** – *go by tram*
- **ехать на мотоцикле** – *go by motorbike*
- **ехать на велосипеде** – *go by bicycle*

When you talk about the destination of movement, use prepositions **в** or **на** followed by the destination noun in the accusative case.

For instance:

Listen to Track 153

- **Я еду в школу (в Россию, в кино, в театр, в спортзал, в магазин).**
  I go to school (to Russia, to the cinema, to the theatre, to the gym, to the shop).

- **Я еду на Ямайку (на концерт, на совещание, на почту).**
  I go to Jamaica (to the concert, to the meeting, to the post office).

We hope it is clear with **идти/ходить** and **ехать/ездить**. But how about other methods of movement?

Russian verbs of motion: 15 more pairs

The first verb in the pair is unidirectional, and it is used for describing a single action. The second one is multidirectional, and it is for habitual, repeated movements:

Listen to Track 154

1. **бежать — бегать (*run*)**
   - Сегодня тяжело **бежать** из-за жары. Я люблю **бегать**, но это уже слишком. – *It's hard to run today because of the heat. I love running, but that's too much.*

2. **лететь — летать (*fly*)**
   - Они будут **лететь** в Москву на следующей неделе. – *They are going to fly to Moscow next week.*
   - Тебе страшно **летать** на самолете? – *Are you scared of flying?*

3. **плыть — плавать** (*swim, sail, float*)

- В задании сказано было **плыть** на другой берег, но я не смогла его выполнить, потому что не умею **плавать**. – *The task was to swim to the other side, but I couldn't complete it because I can't swim.*

Listen to Track 155

4. **катить — катать** (*roll, wheel*)

- У сумки есть колеса, можешь ее просто **катить**. – *The bag has wheels, so you can just roll it.*

- Нужно **катать** этот кусочек теста, пока не получится шарик. – *You need to roll this piece of dough until it becomes round.*

    Катать also means taking somebody for a ride/drive:

- Когда я был маленьким, я любил, когда папа **катал меня на машине.** – *When I was a child, I liked when my dad drove me around in his car.*

5. **катиться — кататься** (*move by rolling, wheeling, or sliding*)

- У малышки по щекам **катились** слезы. – *Tears were rolling down the little girl's cheeks.*

    The multidirectional verb **кататься** means an activity. Since there are lots of means we can use in order to roll, wheel, or slide, the verb **кататься** can be used with different nouns according to this scheme:

6. **кататься + на + noun** (*prep. case*)

    You've got to learn this well because, unlike English, Russian doesn't have unique verbs for different activities associated with the use of various sports or leisure equipment. So you will have to use **кататься на** every time you want to say something like this:

- **кататься на** санках – *to toboggan, to sledge*
- **кататься на** лыжах – *to ski*
- **кататься на** водных лыжах – *to water-ski*
- **кататься на** коньках – *to skate*
- **кататься на** сноуборде – *to snowboard*
- **кататься на** скейтборде – *to skateboard*
- **кататься на** велосипеде – *to (bi)cycle, to ride a bike*
- **кататься на** роликах (роликовых коньках) – *to rollerblade*

Listen to Track 156

7. нести — носить (*carry by foot*)

- Мне нельзя **носить** тяжелое. Ты мог бы по**нести** мой чемодан, пожалуйста? – *I Can't carry heavy things. Would you carry my suitcase please?*

8. везти — возить (*carry by transportation*)

- Сегодня моя очередь **везти** детей в школу. Нам с мужем приходится **возить** их по очереди. – *It's my turn to drive the kids to school. Me and my husband have to drive them in turns.*

9. вести — водить (*lead, take by foot*)

- Узнай, нужно ли **вести** детей в школу. Может, не нужно их **водить**, пока не закончится эпидемия? – *Find out whether we need to take the kids to school. Maybe we shouldn't take them to school until the epidemic is over.*

    This pair of motion verbs is also responsible for driving a car. A driver is Russian is **водитель**.

- Во время снегопада нужно **вести** машину очень осторожно. – *One needs to drive carefully in the snow.*

- Я еще не научился **водить** машину как профи. – *I haven't learned to drive like a pro yet.*

Listen to Track 157

10. тащить — таскать (*drag, pull, carry*)

- **Тащи** это полено к огню. – *Drag this log closer to the fire.*

11. нестись — носиться (*rush [off], run around, dash*)

- Куда вы так **несётесь**? – *Where are you rushing off to?*

- Не люблю, когда моя кошка начинает **носиться** по дому как угорелая. – *I hate when my cat starts to run around the house like a mad thing.*

12. ползти — ползать (*crawl*)

- По стене **ползёт** паук. – *A spider is crawling on the wall.*

- Люди так **ползать** не умеют. – *People can't crawl like that.*

Listen to Track 158

13. лезть — лазить/лазать (*climb*)

- Мне совсем не хотелось **лезть** на это дерево. – *I didn't want to climb this tree at all.*
- В детстве я любил **лазать** по деревьям. – *I loved climbing trees when I was a child.*

14. брести — бродить (*wander, roam, trudge*)

- Они **брели** по лесу часами, пока не вышли на дорогу. – *They had trudged through the woods for hours until they found a road.*
- Я люблю **бродить** по парку после работы. – *I love wandering in the park after work.*

15. гнать — гонять (*drive, turn out*)

- Смотри, пастух **гонит** свою отару через луг. Ему нужно **гонять** ее через этот луг дважды в день. – *Look, a shepherd is driving his herd across the meadow. He has to drive it though this meadow twice a day.*

  Although **гнать/гонять** mean to force somebody to move, they also mean to drive a car in a fast, often reckless manner:

- Ты **гонишь** слишком быстро, мне страшно. – *You are driving too fast, I'm scared.*

16. гнаться — гоняться (*pursue, chase*)

- Смотри, твой пес **гонится** за соседским котом. – *Look, your dog is chasing the neighbor's cat.*
- Ты прав, не знаю, как отучить его **гоняться** за котами. – *You are right, I have no idea how to wean him off of chasing cats.*

Phew, that was a crazy sprint. We dashed through this topic as fast as we can, and we hope you got the gist of the Russian verbs of motion. Now you can talk about your favorite activities and all the other motions that life is full of.

TIME TO PRACTICE!

Exercise 1 - Choose and write:

1. Я ... на футбол каждую пятницу. (*I go to football every Friday.*)

   a) бегаю   b) хожу   c) схожу

2. Сегодня мы ... домой другой дорогой. (*Today we will go home another way.*)

   a) ходим   b) ездим   c) пойдем

3. В детстве я так и не научится ... на велосипеде. (*As a child, I never learned to ride a bike.*)

   a) ехать   b) ездить   c) съездить

4. Новосибирск очень далеко от Москвы. Нужно ... на поезде несколько суток. (*Novosibirsk is very far from Moscow. You need to travel by train for several days.*)

   a) ездить   b) поехать   c) ехать

Exercise 2 - Complete the sentences underlining the correct verb of motion based on their directionality:

1. Мне нравится <u>ходить</u> / идти домой пешком после работы. (*I like to walk home after work.*)

2. Ты будешь ходить / пойдешь сегодня с нами на тренировку? (*Will you go to practice with us today?*)

3. До моей работы нужно ехать / ездить на машине целый час. (*I have to drive an hour to my office.*)

4. Твоя сестра поедет / съездит с нами на пляж? (*Will your sister come to the beach with us?*)

5. Анастасия любит идти / ходить на концерты и выставки. (*Anastasia likes to go to concerts and exhibitions.*)

Exercise 3 - Translate the sentences into Russian paying attention to the directionality of Russian verbs of motion:

1. Children usually go to school by bus.

    _____

2. It's late now. We will take a cab.

    _____

3. I am going to go to the beach by bicycle.

    _____

4. To go by tram is cheaper, but to go by car is faster.

    _____

5. My friend used to go to work by motorbike.

    _____

Exercise 4 - Underline the correct verb:

1. Жаль, что люди не умеют лететь / летать. (*It's a pity that people can't fly.*)
2. В лесу мы увидели медведя, и нам пришлось бегать / бежать. (*In the forest we saw a bear, and we had to run.*)
3. Мы с друзьями хотим поехать / поездить в горы покатиться / покататься на сноуборде. (*My friends and I want to go to the mountains to go snowboarding.*)
4. Мой муж очень хорошо водит / ведет машину. (*My husband is a very good driver.*)
5. Когда я лез / лазил на дерево, мои джинсы порвались. (*When I was climbing a tree, my jeans got torn.*)
6. Мне было трудно плавать / плыть против течения, и я быстро устал. (*It was difficult for me to swim against the current, and I quickly got tired.*)

Exercise 5 - Fill in the table creating pairs of Russian verbs of motion:

Unidirectional	Multidirectional
Лететь (*fly*)	
	Бегать (*run*)
Плыть (*swim*)	
	Катать (*ride*)
Катиться (*roll*)	
	Носить (*wear*)
Везти (*carry*)	
	Таскать (*carry*)
Вести (*lead*)	
	Носиться (*run around*)
Ползти (*crawl*)	
	Лазить (*climb*)
Брести (*wander*)	
	Гонять (*drive*)
Гнаться (*chase*)	

Answers

Exercise 1

1. b 2. c 3. b 4. c

Exercise 2:

2. пойдешь, 3. ехать, 4. поедет, 5. ходить.

Exercise 3

1. Дети обычно ездят в школу на автобусе.
2. Уже поздно. Мы поедем на такси.
3. Я поеду на пляж на велосипеде.
4. Ехать на трамвае дешевле, но ехать на машине быстрее.
5. Мой друг ездил на работу на мотоцикле.

Exercise 4

1. летать, 2. бежать, 3. поехать, покататься, 4. водит, 5. лез, 6. плыть.

Exercise 5

Unidirectional	Multidirectional
Лететь	Летать
Бежать	Бегать
Плыть	Плавать
Катить	Катать
Катиться	Кататься
Нести	Носить
Везти	возить
Тащить	таскать
Вести	водить
Нестись	носиться
Ползти	ползать
Лезть	лазить
Брести	бродить
Гнать	гонять
Гнаться	гоняться

Lesson 15: Russian Adverbs of Place

Today, we are going to get into the nitty-gritty of adverbs of place and the nuances of their use.

Listen to Track 159

You will be surprised to find out that while English uses only one question (*where?*) to ask about all kinds of places, Russian has four: **где? куда? откуда?** and **докуда?**

You will even find this weird fact pretty logical since adverbs of place in Russian indicate not only where the action takes place (**где?**). They also tell where a movement starts from (**откуда?**), where it is directed (**куда?**), and even how far it proceeds (**докуда?**).

This table will help you understand the difference:

Где?	Куда?	Откуда?	Докуда?
Он **тут**. *He is **here**.*	Иди **сюда**. *Come **here**.*	Ему не хочется уходить **отсюда**. *He doesn't want to go **from here**.*	Дойди **досюда** и остановись. *Go **to here** and stop.*
Она **там**. *She is **there**.*	Иди **туда**. *Go **there**.*	Ей не хочется уходить **оттуда**. *She doesn't want to go **from there**.*	Дойди **дотуда** и остановись. *Go to **there** and stop.*

It is much easier to learn Russian adverbs of place by categorizing them into these four question groups. It is because your choice of adverb will be different based on whether the object is stationary (action happens in a particular place) or it is moving (in some direction, from some place, or up to it).

Adverbs of the place of action (Где?)

From asking where the nearest bus station is to asking where your friends live or work, где-questions are probably the most popular ones, especially among tourists. That is why you should know the adverbs of place that help answer this kind of question.

Listen to Track 160

For example:

- Скажите, пожалуйста, где здесь **поблизости** продуктовый магазин? – *Please tell me where there is a grocery **nearby**?*
- Вон **там**, **напротив**. – *It's **over there**, **across the street**.*

Russian adverb	English	Example
тут здесь	*Here*	**Здесь** тихо. *It's quiet **here**.*
там	*There*	**Там** слишком холодно. *It's too cold **there**.*
справа	*on/to the right*	Мой дом **справа**. *My house is **on the right**.*
слева	*on/to the left*	**Слева** вы видите музей. ***On the left**, you can see a museum.*
впереди	*ahead, in front*	Мой брат идет **впереди**. *My brother is walking **ahead/in front of** me.*
спереди	*at the front, in the front*	В кино я люблю сидеть **спереди**. *In the cinema, I like to sit **in the front**.*
сзади	*behind, in the back*	Пёс медленно идет **сзади**. *A dog slowly walks **behind**.*
позади	*Behind*	Нужно оставить все **позади** и жить дальше. *You need to leave it all **behind** and move on.*
вверху	*above, up*	Тебе нужно перейти по ссылке **вверху**. *You need to click the link **above**.*
наверху	*above, up(stairs)*	Моя комната **наверху**. *My room is **upstairs**.*
внизу	*below, down(stairs)*	**Внизу** у реки была лодка. *There was a boat **down** by the lake.*

вокруг	*Around*	**Вокруг** все покрыто снегом. *Everything **around** is covered in snow.*
везде всюду повсюду	*Everywhere*	Мы **везде** искали тебя. *We were looking for you **everywhere**.*
нигде	*nowhere/anywhere*	Я **нигде** не нашел эту книгу. *I haven't found this book **anywhere**.*
негде	*nowhere to*	Так много людей... **Негде** сесть. *So many people. There's **nowhere to** sit.*
дома	*at home*	На выходных я люблю оставаться **дома**. *I like to stay **at home** on weekends.*
напротив	*across, opposite*	Мой друг живет в доме напротив. *My friend lives **across** the street.*
далеко	*far (away)*	Звезды очень **далеко**. *Stars are very **far away**.*
недалеко	*not far*	Автобусная остановка **недалеко**. *The bus stop is **not far**.*
близко	*near(by), close*	Здесь шумно, потому что шоссе очень **близко**. *It's noisy because the motorway is very **close**.*
поблизости	*Nearby*	Здесь **поблизости** есть кафе? *Is there any cafe **nearby**?*
рядом	*beside, next to, nearby, around*	Он идет, а собака бежит **рядом**. *He's walking, and the dog's running **beside** him.*
внутри	*(on the) inside*	**Внутри** дом красивее, чем снаружи. *The house is more beautiful **on the inside** than outside.*
снаружи	*Outside*	Мои друзья ждут меня **снаружи**. *My friends are waiting for me **outside**.*

Adverbs of the direction of movement (Куда?)

Listen to Track 161

The second biggest group of Russian adverbs of place answers the question **Куда?/ Where to?** (direction of movement). We use them for objects that change their location.

For example:

- Куда ты идешь? – *Where are you going?*
- Я иду **домой**. – *I'm heading **home**.*

Russian adverb	English	Example
Сюда	*Here*	Подойдите **сюда**. *Come **here**.*
Туда	*There*	Я очень хочу поехать **туда**. *I want to go **there** very much.*
вперёд	*forward, ahead*	Иди **вперёд**, я догоню. *Go **ahead**, I'll catch you up.*
Назад	*back(ward)*	Нам нужно вернуться **назад**. *We need to go **back**.*
Вверх	*Up*	Руки **вверх**! *Hands **up**!*
Наверх	*up(ward, stairs)*	Посмотрите **наверх**. *Look **upward**.*
Вниз	*down(ward, stairs)*	Макс собирается прыгнуть с дерева **вниз**. *Max is going to jump **down** from the tree.*
направо	*right, to the right*	Автобус повернул **направо**. *The bus turned **right**.*
Налево	*left, to the left*	Посмотри **налево**. *Look **to the left**.*
Прямо	*Straight*	Мне было трудно научиться ехать на велосипеде **прямо**. *It was hard for me to learn to ride my bike **straight**.*

Мимо	*past, by*	Он прошел **мимо,** не заметив меня .
		*He went **by** without noticing me.*
Внутрь	*in(side)*	На улице холодно, давай зайдем **внутрь.**
		*It's cold. Let's get **inside.***
наружу	*out(side)*	Котенок не хотел сидеть в коробке и пытался выбраться **наружу.**
		*The kitten didn't like sitting in a box and tried to come **out.***
(не)далеко	*(not) far (away)*	Мяч улетел **далеко.**
		*The ball flew **far away.***
обратно	*Back*	Мне нужно слетать по работе в Москву и **обратно.**
		*I need to fly to Moscow and **back** for my work.*
никуда	*nowhere, anywhere*	Она **никуда** не хочет ехать.
		*She doesn't want to go **anywhere.***

Adverbs of the starting point of movement (Откуда?)

Listen to Track 162

In English, when the object is moving from some place, we use the preposition **from** to create various sources of movement. That's all. "That's too simple," Russians thought, and created over 10 original adverbs that describe the starting point of action and answer the question **Откуда?/Where (from)?**

Russian adverb	English	Example
отсюда	*from here*	Мне не хочется уходить **отсюда**. *I don't want to go **from here**.*
Оттуда	*from there*	**Оттуда** слышался смех и веселые крики. *Laughs and shouts of joy were heard **from there**.*
Сверху	*from above*	Мне нравится смотреть на облака **сверху**, когда я лечу на самолете. *I like to look at the clouds **from above** when I fly by plane.* **Сверху вниз** - *from top to bottom.*
Снизу	*from below,* *from (the) bottom*	Небоскребы выглядят гигантскими, если смотреть на них **снизу**. *The skyscrapers look huge when you look at them **from below**.*
отовсюду	*from everywhere*	В Москву съезжаются туристы **отовсюду**. *Tourists come to Moscow from **everywhere**.*
издали = издалека	*from afar*	Я узнал тебя **издалека**. *I recognized you **from afar**.*
изнутри	*from (the) inside*	Эта дверь открывается **изнутри**. *This door opens **from the inside**.*
снаружи	*from (the) outside*	**Снаружи** не видно, что там внутри. *You can't see what's inside **from the outside**.*
ниоткуда	*from nowhere/* *anywhere, out of* *nowhere*	Эти парни появились из **ниоткуда** и все испортили. *These guys came **out of nowhere** and ruined everything.*
Неоткуда (= негде)	*nowhere to... from*	Им **неоткуда** брать информацию. *There's **nowhere** they can take information **from**.*

The list of Russian adverbs of place doesn't end here. Russians invented one more creative way to produce them—using particles. We couldn't ignore this big group of adverbs since they are far too frequent in everyday communication to omit them.

-то, -либо, -нибудь, and кое- adverbs of place

Sometimes in a conversation, we don't want to be precise about the place. Or we cannot be precise because we don't know the place. There's a group of Russian adverbs that help you keep it vague or general. They are formed by adding particles -то, -либо, -нибудь, or кое- to the question words где, куда, and откуда. (Forming them from докуда is also technically possible, but it's a rare case, so we omit it).

1. Где-то, куда-то, откуда-то

The particle -то points to an exact place or direction you don't know.

Listen to Track 163

Где-то can be translated as **somewhere** (in affirmative sentences) or as **anywhere** (in negative and interrogative sentences):

- Нам нужно **где-то** остановиться и перекусить.– *We need to stop* **somewhere** *and grab a bite.*
- Ты **где-то** видел мой телефон? – *Have you seen my cell phone* **anywhere**?
- Он **куда-то** ушел. – *He went* **somewhere**.
- **Откуда-то** сверху лился свет. – *The light was pouring* **from somewhere** *above.*

2. Где-либо, куда-либо, откуда-либо

Listen to Track 164

The particle -либо means **anywhere** (any place at all):

- Родители не разрешают мне гулять **где-либо** поздно вечером. – *My parents don't let me go out* **anywhere** *late in the evening.*
- Я устал и не хочу идти сегодня **куда-либо** еще. – *I'm tired and don't want to go* **anywhere** *else today.*
- Он не ожидал, что ему позвонят **откуда-либо** сегодня, поэтому выключил телефон. – *He didn't expect calls from* **anywhere** *today, so he switched his phone off.*

3. Где-нибудь, куда-нибудь, откуда-нибудь

Listen to Track 165

The particle **-нибудь** means that there are a few options of place, but the exact location isn't important:

- Давай **где-нибудь** поужинаем вместе! – *Let's dine **somewhere** together!*
- Ты был **где-нибудь** за границей? – *Have you been **anywhere** abroad?*
- Мне хочется **куда-нибудь** съездить в эти выходные. – *I want to go **somewhere** this weekend.*
- Позвони мне **откуда-нибудь**, когда будешь на месте. – *Call me from **somewhere** when you are there.*

4. Кое-где, кое-куда, кое-откуда

Listen to Track 166

The particle **кое-** means that you know the exact place but want to keep it a secret for some reason. We can translate it as "someplace":

- Я спешу, мне нужно в полдень быть **кое-где**. – *I'm in a hurry, I need to be **somewhere** at noon.*
- По дороге домой мне нужно **кое-куда** заскочить. – *I need to stop **someplace** on the way home.*
- Где ты взял такой блокнот? Отец привез его мне **кое-откуда**. – *Where did you get this notebook? My dad brought it for me from **someplace**.*

Congrats, that's the finish line. You have just learned lots of Russian adverbs of place, so now, in a conversation, you can be very particular about the place — or just the opposite, keep it vague. We recommend practising these adverbs in a context, and the best way to do so is to try out our exercises.

TIME TO PRACTICE!

Exercise 1 - Put these adverbs into the correct box depending on their question:

Назад, наверху, изнутри, дотуда, издали, откуда-то, отовсюду, налево, сверху, где-либо, поблизости, напротив, досюда, ниоткуда, мимо, туда, домой.

Где? (Where?)	Куда? (Where to?)	Откуда? (where from?)	Докуда? (How far?)

Exercise 2 - Choose the correct adverbs and complete the sentences:

1. Продуктовый магазин (вперед, нигде, недалеко, внутри). – The *grocery store is nearby.*

   _____

2. (Там, везде, отовсюду, поблизости) дождь, не забудь зонт. - *It's raining — don't forget your umbrella.*

   _____

3. Мне нравится идти с тобой (спереди, рядом, издалека, где-нибудь) и держать тебя за руку. - *I like to walk beside you and hold your hand.*

   _____

4. Езжайте (назад, вверх, наружу, прямо), потом поверните (внутрь, налево, мимо). - *Drive straight, then turn left.*

   _____

5. (Дома, поблизости, здесь) очень много людей, давай выйдем (наверх, налево, наружу).- *There are a lot of people here. Let's go outside.*

   _____

Exercise 3 - Correct the errors. Change the adverbs used in these sentences to a more appropriate one:

1. Ты хотела бы где-то сходить сегодня вечером? - *Would you like to go somewhere tonight?*

2. Какая красивая коробка! Давай заглянем внутри! - *What a beautiful box! Let's take a look inside!*

3. Я забыл телефон, поэтому теперь возвращаюсь позади. - *I forgot my phone, so now I'm going back.*

4. У тебя дома нигде присесть, нет ни одного стула.- *You have no place to sit at home — there is not a single chair.*

5. Маше никуда-либо не хочется идти в такую погоду. - *Masha does not want to go anywhere in this weather.*

6. Уходите отовсюду, не то я вызову полицию! - *Get out of here, or I'll call the police!*

7. Когда закончишь делать уроки, спускайся снизу поужинать.- *When you finish your homework, go down to dinner.*

Exercise 4 - Choose the adverb with the correct particle:

1. Мария (куда-нибудь, куда-то, куда-либо) ушла, скоро вернется. - *Maria went somewhere but will be back soon.*

2. Путешествовать (кое-куда, куда-то, куда-либо, куда-нибудь) на машине намного удобнее и быстрее, чем поездом. - *Traveling anywhere by car is much more convenient and faster than by train.*

3. Я (где-нибудь, кое-где, где-либо, где-то) оставил свой рюкзак, и мне нужно за ним заехать. - *I left my backpack somewhere, and I need to pick it up.*

4. Жилье в маленьком городе намного дешевле, чем (где-либо, где-то, кое-где, где-нибудь) в Москве. - *Housing in a small city is much cheaper than anywhere else in Moscow.*

5. Мне неожиданно (кое-откуда, откуда-нибудь, откуда-то) пришла посылка сегодня утром. - *I suddenly received a package from somewhere this morning.*

Answers

Exercise 1

Где?	Куда?	Откуда?	Докуда?
Наверху	назад	Изнутри	Дотуда
Сверху	налево	откуда-то	Досюда
где-либо	мимо	Отовсюду	
Поблизости	туда	Издали	
Напротив	домой	Ниоткуда	

Exercise 2

1. Недалеко 2. Там 3. Рядом 4. Прямо, налево 5. Здесь, наружу.

Exercise 3

1. Куда-то 2. Внутрь 3. Назад 4. Негде 5. Никуда 6. Отсюда 7. Вниз

Exercise 4

1. Куда-то 2. Куда-либо 3. Кое-где 4. Где-нибудь 5. Откуда-то

Lesson 16: Question Words in Russian

In Russian, we form questions in a slightly different way than in English. First of all, we don't have auxiliary verbs (*do, be,* or *have*) to make questions. Instead, we easily turn a statement into a question by pronouncing it with a rising intonation.

Another way to form a question in Russian is with the use of various question words (pronouns and adverbs). What are they, when do we use them, and how do we make them agree with other words in a question? Let's get everything straight!

The most frequently used Russian question words

Listen to Track 167

- **Кто? – *Who?***

  Кто будет вести урок сегодня? – ***Who** is going to teach today?*

  Кому мороженного? – ***Who** wants some ice cream?*

- **Что? (pronounce it: shtoh) – *What?***

  Что случилось? – ***What** happened?*

  Чего здесь не хватает? – ***What** is missing here?*

- **Какой? – *What kind of? What? Which?***

  Какие книги ты обычно берешь в библиотеке? – ***What kind of** books do you usually take from the library?*

  На **какой** улице ты живешь? – ***What** street do you live on?*

  Какой оттенок тебе нравится больше? – ***Which** tint do you like most?*

- **Который? – *Which one? What? (for asking time)***

  Который час? – ***What** time is it?*

  Которое из этих платьев мне больше идет? – ***Which one** of these dresses looks better on me?*

- **Чей? –** *Whose?*

  Чья это сумка? – ***Whose*** *bag is that?*

  Чьи лекции тебе понравились больше всего? – ***Whose*** *lectures did you like most?*

- **Где? –** *Where?*

  We use it when we want to know the exact place:

  Где сегодня будет вечеринка? – ***Where*** *is the party going to be tonight?*

- **Куда? –** *Where (to)?*

  We use it to find out the direction of motion:

  Куда едет этот поезд? – ***Where*** *is the train going?*

Listen to Track 168

- **Откуда? –** *Where (from)? How?*

  We use it to find out the starting point of motion or the source of something:

  Откуда у тебя столько идей? – ***Where*** *do you get all those ideas* ***from***?

  Откуда он знает, что сегодня твой день рождения? – ***How*** *does he know it's your birthday today?*

- **Сколько? –** *How many? How much?*

  Сколько сахара положить тебе в чай? – ***How much*** *sugar do you want in your tea?*

  Сколько тебе лет? – ***How*** *old are you?*

  Сколькими языками ты свободно владеешь? – ***How many*** *languages do you speak fluently?*

- **Насколько?** – *To what extent? How...?*

  Насколько хорошо вы говорите по-русски? – *How well do you speak Russian?*

  Насколько ты нуждаешься в помощи переводчика? – *To what extent do you need an interpreter?*

- **Как?** – *How?*

  Как твои дела? – *How do you do?*

  Как ты собираешься добраться туда без машины? – *How are you going to get there without a car?*

- **Почему?** – *Why? How come?*

  Почему в русском языке так много падежей? – *Why are there so many cases in Russian?*

  Почему твой брат до сих пор не женат? – *How come your brother never married until now?*

- **Зачем?** – *Why? What for?*

  We often use it to find out the intention/purpose of an action or to express regret or doubt:

  Зачем ты позвал меня сюда? – *What did you call me here for?*

  Зачем тратить на это время, если это бесполезно? – *Why waste time on it if it's pointless?*

- **Можно?** – *Can? May?*

  It is a polite manner to ask for permission to do something:

  Алло, здравствуйте, **можно** поговорить с Катей? – *Hello, may I talk to Katya?*

  Можно мне еще воды, пожалуйста? – *May I have some more water, please?*

  Можно одолжить твой телефон на секунду? – *Can I borrow your cellphone for a second?*

We hope you have noticed some very important details when reading these examples. Question words **кто, что,** and **сколько** inflect for cases, while **какой** and **чей** also inflect for gender and number. Please keep reading to find out how it happens in detail.

Кто, что, and сколько

Listen to Track 169

The interrogative words **кто** (*who*) and **что** (*what*) are pronouns. **Кто** is used to ask about animate referents (people or animals), while **что** points to inanimate referents.

These question words are easy to deal with because they don't care too much about the number and gender of predicates they go with. **Кто** and **что** adjust them to themselves.

So, regardless of the predicate's gender and number, they must be put into masculine singular for **кто**:

- Кто **выпил** мой кофе? (Выпил–m, sing.) – *Who has drunk my coffee?*

...and into neuter singular for **что**:

- Что **помогло** тебе пройти через эти трудности? (помогло–n, sing.) – *What helped you to get through these difficulties?*

Since the adverb **сколько** (*how many / how much*) is needed to find out the quantity, it automatically puts the noun in a sentence into plural:

- Сколько **детей** сегодня было на уроке? (детей–plur.) – *How many kids were in class today?*

Declension of кто, что, and сколько

Listen to Track 170

As you remember, there are six grammar cases in the Russian language. Pronouns **кто** and **что,** as well as the adverb **сколько,** inflect for all of them:

Case	кто	что	сколько
Nominative	кто	что	сколько
Genitive	кого	чего	скольких
Dative	кому	чему	скольким
Accusative	кого	что	сколько
Instrumental	кем	чем	сколькими
Prepositional	о ком	о чём	о скольких

According to animate/inanimate declension rules we have already talked about in our chapter about Russian adjectives, **кто** has the same forms for genitive and accusative cases, while **что** and **сколько** have the same forms for nominative and accusative.

Какой, который, чей

Listen to Track 171

Какой (*what kind of*) is also a pronoun. We use it when we want to ask about the quality of a thing or a person. **Какой** always agrees with a noun in case, number, and gender:

Case	Masculine	Feminine	Neuter	Plural
Nominative	какой	какая	какое	какие
Genitive	какого	какой	какого	каких
Dative	какому	какой	какому	каким
Accusative	какого (anim.) какой (inanim.)	какую	какое	каких (anim.) какие (inanim.)
Instrumental	каким	какой	каким	какими
Prepositional	о каком	о какой	о каком	о каких

Listen to Track 172

The pronoun **который** (*which one/what*) helps us ask about a single object in a sequence of similar objects. This is how it inflects for the case, gender, and number:

Case	Masculine	Feminine	Neuter	Plural
Nominative	который	которая	Которое	которые
Genitive	которого	которой	Которого	которых
Dative	которому	которой	Которому	которым
Accusative	которого (anim.) который (inanim.)	которую	Которое	которых (anim.) которые (inanim.)
Instrumental	которым	которой	Которым	которыми
Prepositional	о котором	о которой	о котором	о которых

Listen to Track 173

Чей is used when we want to find out whom something belongs to. Since it is also a pronoun, we need to make **чей** agree with a noun it refers to. Here is how:

Case	Masculine	Feminine	Neuter	Plural
Nominative	чей	чья	Чьё	чьи
Genitive	чьего	чьей	Чьего	чьих
Dative	чьему	чьей	Чьему	чьим
Accusative	чьего (anim.) чей (inanim.)	чью	Чьё	чьих (anim.) чьи (inanim.)
Instrumental	чьим	чьей	Чьим	чьими
Prepositional	о чьём	о чьей	о чьём	о чьих

Declension of Russian pronouns is difficult. Especially the last table can be tough for those who have just started to learn Russian and to get used to its weird pronunciation. But do not let it upset you.

Time and practice make perfect.

So take your time with these question words and don't forget to reinforce what you just learned with our exercises!

TIME TO PRACTICE!

Exercise 1 - Fill in the gaps, choosing the correct question word:

1. ... ты учишь иностранные языки? (... *do you learn foreign languages?*)

    a) Сколько   b) Зачем   c) Откуда

2. ... Вы научились так хорошо играть на гитаре? (... *did you learn to play the guitar so well?*)

    a) Почему   b) Где   c) Кого

3. ... упражнений было в домашнем задании? (... *exercises were there in the homework?*)

    a) Сколько   b) Сколько стоит c) Которые

4. ... попросить у тебя ручку на секундочку? (... *borrow your pen for a second?*)

    a) Почему   b) Как   c) Можно

5. ... ты положил мой кошелек? (... *did you put my wallet?*)

    a) Откуда   b) Где   c) Куда

6. ... ты родом? (... *are you from?*)

    a) Откуда   b) Где   c) Куда

7. ... вы пойдете ужинать сегодня? (... *are you going for dinner tonight?*)

    a) Откуда   b) Где   c) Куда

Exercise 2 - Put the question word in brackets into the correct form according to the case, gender, and number:

1. О (что) вы говорили за завтраком? (*What did you talk about at breakfast?*)

    _____

2. (Кто) ты хочешь стать, когда вырастешь? (*What do you want to be when you grow up?*)

    _____

3. (Сколько) учеников сегодня не было на уроке? (*How many students weren't in class today?*)

    _____

4. (Кто) ты пишешь письмо? (*Who are you writing a letter to?*)

    _____

5. (Сколько) друзей было у тебя на дне рождения? (*How many friends did you have at your birthday party?*)

6. (Сколько) новых русских слов ты сегодня выучил? (*How many new Russian words have you learned today?*)

Exercise 3 - The question words in brackets are in their initial form. Make them agree with the rest of the sentence in case, gender, and number:

1. (Какой) курточку ты сегодня наденешь: синюю или серую? (*What jacket will you wear today – blue or gray?*)

2. (Который) из этих книг ты начнешь читать первой? (*Which of these books will you start reading first?*)

3. О (чей) ребенке идет речь? (*Whose child are we talking about?*)

4. (Какой) языки ты знаешь? (*What languages do you know?*)

5. (Чей) картины вам больше всего понравились в музее?(*Whose paintings did you like most in the museum?*)

6. (Какой) буквы здесь не хватает? (*What letter is missing here?*)

7. (Какой) числа приезжает твой отец? (*What date is your father coming?*)

Exercise 4 - Insert the correct question words, paying attention to whether the referent is animate or inanimate:

Каких, какие

1. ... наушники тебе подарили? (*What headphones did they give you?*)

_____

2. ... домашних животных ты бы хотел иметь дома? (*What kind of pets would you like to have at home?*)

_____

Чей, чьего

3. ... щенка вы вчера катали на велосипеде? (*Whose puppy did you take on your bike yesterday?*)

_____

4. ... это чемодан ты несешь? (*Whose suitcase are you carrying?*)

_____

Который, которого

5. ... парня ты хотела бы поцеловать? (*Which guy would you like to kiss?*)

_____

6. ... рюкзак она брала с собой в поход? (*Which backpack did she take with her on the hike?*)

_____

Чьи, чьих

7. ... цитаты ты использовал в сочинении? (*Whose quotes did you use in your essay?*)

_____

8. ... родителей вызвал в школу директор?(*Whose parents were called to the school by the principal?*)

_____

Exercise 5 - Translate these sentences into Russian, using the question words you learned today:

1. How many years have you known Pavel? – _____
2. Where is your sister going for a vacation? – _____
3. Where did you buy this T-shirt? – _____
4. How much does this car cost? – _____
5. What are you learning Russian for? – _____

Answers

Exercise 1

1. b 2. b 3. a 4. c 5. c 6. a 7. c

Exercise 2

1. Чём 2. Кем 3. Скольких 4. Кому 5. Сколько 6. Сколько

Exercise 3

1. Какую 2. Которую 3. Чьём 4. Какие 5. Чьи 6. Какой 7. Какого

Exercise 4

1. Какие 2. Каких 3. Чьего 4. Чей 5. Которого 6. Который 7. Чьи 8. Чьих

Exercise 5

1. Сколько лет ты знаешь Павла?
2. Куда твоя сестра поедет в отпуск?
3. Где ты купил эту футболку?
4. Сколько стоит эта машина?
5. Зачем ты учишь русский?

Lesson 17: Describing People in Russian

We are always describing. Whether it is people, objects, or weather, we give characteristics all the time, even without noticing it. If objects (and weather) don't really care what we say about them, we should be extra careful when describing people. In this lesson, we will give you some basic nouns, adjectives, and ready-to-use phrases to help you always find the right words when describing appearance or personality.

Describing appearance in Russian

Listen to Track 174

Before we talk about how to answer the question "What does he/she look like?", we should answer the question "Who?" ("**Кто**?") first.

WHO are we actually talking about?

- **Мужчина** – *man*
- **Женщина** – *woman*
- **Парень** – *guy*
- **Молодой человек** – *young man*
- **Девушка** – *girl, a young lady*
- **Ребенок** – *child*
- **Мальчик** – *boy*
- **Девочка** – *girl*
- **Молодой** – *young*
- **Пожилой** – *old*
- **Пожилая женщина** – *old (elderly) woman*
- **Средних лет** – *middle-aged*
- **Преклонного возраста** – *elderly*
- **Старый** – *old*

  (you should be careful with the word "старый" because it is too straightforward and may sound rude).
- **Старик** – *old man*

When we want to find out what somebody looks like, we ask:

- **Как он/она выглядит?** – *What does he/she look like?*

Listen to Track 175

Внешний вид (*appearance*)

This is how we can describe the appearance of a person in general:

- **Красивый** – *handsome, pretty*
- **Милый, миловидный** – *lovely*
- **Симпатичный** – *good-looking*
- **Привлекательный** – *attractive*
- **Хорошенькая** (fem.) – *pretty*
- **Некрасивый, уродливый** – *ugly*
- **Красотка** – *pretty woman*
- **Красавец** – *handsome man*

Also, when we want to describe our first impression, we use the phrase:

Listen to Track 176

"**У** (*person*) (*adjective*) **вид**".

For example:

- **У нее усталый вид.** – *She looks tired.*
- **У этого мужчины ухоженный вид.** – *This man looks well-groomed.*

You can also use other adjectives to describe how a person looks:

- **Неряшливый** – *slovenly*
- **(не)аккуратный** – *(un)tidy*
- **Отталкивающий, неприятный** – *unpleasant*
- **Умный** – *intelligent*
- **Ужасный** – *awful*
- **Ничтожный, жалкий** – *miserable*
- **Внушающий уважение** – *respected*
- **Здоровый** – *healthy*
- **Сногсшибательный** – *stunning*
- *Отдохнувший* – *rested*

For example:

- Она красотка.
- Он симпатичный парень, но у него очень неаккуратный вид.
- Она красивая, ухоженная женщина.
- Это элегантный мужчина с видом, внушающим уважение.
- У тебя усталый вид.

Listen to Track 177

When describing appearance, we can also use the verb выглядеть with an adjective in the instrumental case or an adverb.

For example:

- Ребенок выглядит здоровым.
- Ты отлично (здорово, хорошо, прекрасно, сногсшибательно, шикарно) выглядишь!
- Она выглядит сногсшибательно!

Now we move from a rather emotional description to particular details in appearance.

Listen to Track 178

Рост и фигура (*height and physical shape*)

- **Высокий** – *tall*
- **Невысокий** – *not very tall*
- **Низкий (низенький)** – *short*
- **Высокого / низкого (низенького) / среднего роста** – *tall / short / of average height*
- **Мускулистый, накачанный** – *muscle, buff*
- **Подтянутый, стройный** – *fit*
- **Атлетической внешности** – *athletic*
- **Сильный, крепкий** – *strong*
- **Крепкого телосложения** – *strongly built, of sound physic*
- **Широкоплечий** – *broad-shouldered*
- **Худой (худенький)** – *skinny*

- **Миниатюрный** – *petite*
- **Хрупкий** – *frail*
- **Полный** – *plus-size, fat*
- **Сутулый** – *stooped*
- **Коренастый, приземистый** – *stocky*

For example:

- Это был подтянутый, ухоженный мужчина средних лет.
- Моя сестра — хорошенькая миниатюрная девочка.
- Моя девушка худенькая и низенького роста.

Please note that adjectives with suffixes **-еньк** (like худенький, низенький, старенький) sound more delicate and help soften the characteristic.

Listen to Track 179

Цвет кожи (*skin colour*)

- **Светлокожий** – *fair-skinned*
- **Темнокожий, смуглый** – *dark-skinned*
- **Загорелый** – *tan*

For example:

- Евгений — высокий загорелый парень атлетической внешности.
- Наташа выглядит отдохнувшей и загорелой.

Listen to Track 180

Волосы (*hair*)

- **Короткие** – *short*
- **Длинные** – *long*
- **Средней длинны** – *medium length*
- **Прямые** – *straight*
- **Волнистые, вьющиеся** – *wavy*
- **Кудрявые** – *curly*

The same word in its singular form can be used as a characteristic of a person:

- Он кудрявый парень.
- Она кудрявая загорелая девчонка.

Other hair characteristics:

- **Густые** – *thick*
- **Редкие** – *thin*
- **Взъерошенные** – *tousled*
- **Уложенные** – *coiffed*
- **Блестящие** – *glossy*

Listen to Track 181

How about the hair color?

- **Русые** – *dark blonde (light brown)*
- **Темно-русые, каштановые** – *brown hair*
- **Светлые** – *fair*
- **Темные** – *dark*
- **Черные** – *black*
- **Рыжие** – *red*
- **Седые** – *grey*
- **Окрашенные** – *dyed*

Depending on the hair colour, we can characterize a person as:

- **Брюнет** (masc.)/ **брюнетка** (fem.) – *brunette*
- **Блондин / блондинка** – *blonde*
- **Шатен / шатенка** – *brown-haired*
- **Темноволосый** – *dark-haired*
- **Светловолосый** – *blonde-haired*
- **Рыжеволосый** – *red-haired*
- **Седовласый** – *white-haired*

For example:

- Он симпатичный молодой человек с короткими, темными, вьющимися волосами.
- Анна — невысокая светлокожая брюнетка с короткими прямыми волосами.
- У неё длинные седые волосы.
- У моей сестры густые каштановые волосы.
- Светлана — стройная блондинка средних лет.

Listen to Track 182

Глаза (*eyes*)

- **Большие** – *big*
- **Маленькие** – *small*
- **Добрые** – *kind*
- **Сияющие** – *twinkling*
- **Карие** – *brown*
- **Черные** – *black*
- **Голубые** – *blue*
- **Зелёные** – *green*
- **Серые** – *grey*

Listen to Track 183

If we want to describe the manner in which a person looks at something with their eyes, we use the word **взгляд** (*look/eyes*) and adjectives like:

- **Хмурый (взгляд)** – *frown*
- **Нежный** – *tender*
- **Серьезный** – *serious*
- **Робкий, застенчивый** – *shy*
- **Строгий** – *strict*
- **Тяжелый** – *hard*
- **Радостный** – *cheerful*
- **Задумчивый** – *thoughtful, faraway*
- **Хитрый** – *sly*

You can also use these adjectives to characterize the eyes directly.

Examples:

- У него большие голубые глаза и задумчивый взгляд.
- Это девочка с большими карими глазами и хитрым взглядом.
- У старика были добрые серые глаза.
- Это мужчина с маленькими темными глазами и тяжелым взглядом.

Listen to Track 184

Улыбка (*smile*)

- **Радостная** – *happy*
- **Тёплая** – *warm*
- **Широкая** – *wide*
- **Неестественная** – *forced*
- **Обворожительная** – *charming*
- **Застенчивая** – *shy*
- **Приветливая, дружелюбная** – *friendly*

Examples:

- Это девушка невысокого роста с большими сияющими глазами и обворожительной улыбкой.
- У Ивана короткие темные волосы, красивые голубые глаза и дружелюбная улыбка.

Listen to Track 185

Лицо (*face*)

- **Гладко выбритое** – *clean-shaven*
- **Небритое** – *unshaved*
- **Борода** – *beard*
- **Длинная** – *long*
- **Короткая бородка** – *goatee*
- **Бородатый** – *beardy*

- **Усы** – *moustache*
- **Усатый** – *with a big moustache*

For example:

- Мы встретили высокого усатого мужчину.
- У моего отца густая черная борода.

We've tried to describe the most important parts of human appearance. We couldn't cover all possible details like the form of ears or mouth, for example, but this list of words and expressions is a good start. Now we move on to the person on the inside.

Describing personality in Russian

By personality, we mean the person's character, manners, and the impression they make.

Listen to Track 186

- **Добрый** – *kind*
- **Злой** – *angry*
- **Открытый** – *open*
- **Вежливый** – *courteous*
- **Спокойный** – *quiet*
- **Приветливый, дружелюбный** – *friendly*
- **Приятный в общении** – *pleasant, nice to talk to*
- **Беззаботный** – *easygoing*
- **Стеснительный** – *shy*
- **Терпеливый** – *patient*
- **Амбициозный** – *ambitious*
- **Умный** – *intelligent*
- **Весёлый** – *funny*
- **Ленивый** – *lazy*
- **Грубый, грубиян** – *rude*
- **Воспитанный** – *well-behaved*
- **Невоспитанный, плохо воспитанный** – *ill-mannered*
- **Непослушный** – *naughty*
- **Ответственный** – *responsible*

- **Безответственный** – *irresponsible*
- **Компанейский, общительный, душа компании** – *sociable*
- **Серьезный** – *serious*
- **Любознательный** – *curious*
- **Жестокий** – *cruel*
- **Подлый** – *mean*
- **Трудолюбивый** – *hardworking*
- **Опытный** – *experienced*
- **Талантливый** – *talented*
- **Скромный** – *humble*
- **Наглый** – *brazen*
- **Надменный** – *arrogant*
- **Взволнованный** – *worried*
- **Заинтересованный** – *interested*
- **Требовательный** – *demanding*
- **Заботливый** – *caring*

For example:

- Люда очень ответственный и опытный сотрудник. А еще она душа компании.
- Никита — весёлый шутник, но он очень ленивый и безответственный.
- Саша очень вежливая и приятная в общении.
- Евгения скромная и застенчивая, но очень талантливая.

Now you have a good base for describing people. We hope you meet only good people on your way, but with all people, remember to always seek the best in them.

Practice makes perfect, so don't forget to check out the exercises we prepared for this topic. They will help you train your describing muscles and become a real compliment guru.

TIME TO PRACTICE!

Exercise 1 - Describe your own appearance (hair, eyes, skin, physical shape, and general appearance) in Russian.

Follow our example:

Я высокий парень двадцати лет с короткими, прямыми, черными волосами, карими глазами и смуглой кожей. Я не красавец, но у меня приятное лицо и широкая улыбка. Я выгляжу здоровым и подтянутым.

Я...

_____

_____

_____

_____

Exercise 2 - Fill in the gaps to make this description true for your close friend:

Моего друга зовут ... . Он ... роста, но ... . У него ... ... волосы, ... глаза и ... кожа. Петя ... и ... . Он очень ... в общении, ... и ... .

_____

_____

_____

Exercise 3 - Fill in the gaps with adjectives or adverbs that fit the context:

1. Ника очень ... девушка, потому что ведет здоровый образ жизни и занимается спортом.

   _____

2. У Светланы ... кожа, потому что она много бывает на солнце.

   _____

3. У Никиты очень ... вид, потому что он целый день много работал.

   _____

4. Ты выглядишь ... в этом платье. Оно тебе очень идет.

   _____

5. У него был ... вид в том старом, изношенном пальто. Мне так его жаль!

_____

6. В этих очках у тебя очень ... вид.

_____

7. Она уже не ..., а скорее ... возраста.

_____

8. Мой брат немного ..., потому что злоупотребляет фастфудом.

_____

9. У него были ... волосы, как будто он их сто лет не расчесывал.

_____

Exercise 4 - Make up positive characteristics to balance the negative ones. Follow our example: _Он не очень талантливый, но ответственный._

1. Мария неопытная, но ...   — _____
2. Анатолий ленивый, но ...   — _____
3. Гриша грубый, но ...   — _____
4. Анастасия надменная, но ...   — _____
5. Виктор требовательный, но ... — _____

Exercise 5 - Now it's time for the compliments. Find positive adjectives to give an imaginary person compliments about his/her:

Лицо, нос, фигура, волосы, глаза, улыбка.

For example: _У тебя очень милое лицо._

_____

_____

_____

Answers

Exercise 1

Exercise 2

Моего друга зовут Петя. Он невысокого роста, но крепкого телосложения. У него красивые волнистые светлые волосы, большие зеленые глаза и светлая кожа. Петя сильный и широкоплечий. Он очень приятный в общении, веселый и дружелюбный.

Exercise 3

1. Стройная (сильная, подтянутая) / 2. Загорелая (смуглая) / 3. Усталый / 4. Шикарно / 5. Жалкий / 6. Умный / 7. Молодая, преклонного / 8.Полный / 9. Взъерошенные.

Exercise 4

1. Терпеливая / 2. Компанейский / 3. Умный / 4. Веселая / 5. Заботливый

Exercise 5

1. У тебя очень приятное лицо. / 2. У тебя очень аккуратный нос. / 3. У Вас очень красивая фигура. / 4. У тебя шикарные волосы. / 5. У Вас очень добрые глаза. / 6.У тебя обворожительная улыбка.

Lesson 18: Asking and Talking About Places in Russian

The English word *"where"* can be translated into Russian as **где**, **куда**, and **откуда**. Not only does Russian have different question words for the location and the direction of movement, but it also uses very specific prepositions driven by different cases. In this article, we will explain how to ask and talk about places and positions in Russian while a later chapter will be devoted to asking and giving directions.

Где? is how we ask about the place

Listen to Track 187

Где? is a favorite question of travellers who come to visit Russia. You'd better memorize it very well because you will need it so many times! For example:

- **Где находится Красная площадь?** – *Where is Red Square?*
- **Где здесь ближайшая станция метро?** – *Where is the closest metro station?*
- **Где здесь уборная?** – *Where is the WC?*

Even if you don't need to navigate a big city like Moscow, you will still use **где?** in your everyday life very often. Most frequently, we use it for the verbs **быть, жить,** and **находиться**.

For example:

- **Где мой телефон?** – *Where's my cell phone?*

You don't see the verb **быть** in this question, but it is there (in our mind). The point is that in Russian, we omit the verb **быть** in sentences in the present tense. So when we want to ask where something is, we just skip the verb and name the object we are looking for.

Not "**Где есть твоя тетрадь?**" but "**Где твоя тетрадь?**"

Other examples of **где**:

- **Где ты живёшь?** – *Where do you live?*
- **Где находится кабинет номер три?** – *Where's room number three (located)?*

The verb **находиться** is used for finding out the direct location of static objects and places. It is not suitable for movable things like your belongings, for example.

Talking about places

В (*in, at*) and **на** (*at, on*) are the most frequently used prepositions that help define a location. They both require the prepositional case.

В (*in, at*)

Listen to Track 188

We use **в**:

1. When the object is located inside something or when we talk about a city, country, etc. (the equivalent of English "in"):
   - Овощи **в** холодильнике. – *Vegetables are **in** the fridge.*
   - Мои книги **в** рюкзаке. – *My books are **in** the backpack.*
   - Я живу **в** Москве. – *I live **in** Moscow.*
   - Мой брат живет **в** Нью-Йорке. – *My brother lives **in** New York.*

2. When the object is located in an enclosed space (the equivalent of English "at"):
   - Маша работает **в** Большом театре. – *Masha works **at** Bolshoi Theatre.*

Places that always require the preposition **в** are:

Listen to Track 189

Russian	English	в + Prep. case
Театр	*theatre*	в театре
кино	*cinema*	в кино
Ресторан	*restaurant*	в ресторане
Аптека	*pharmacy*	в аптеке
Банк	*bank*	в банке
Парк	*park*	в парке
гостиница, отель	*hotel*	в гостинице, в отеле
Музей	*museum*	в музее
Школа	*school*	в школе
Больница	*hospital*	в больнице
Квартира	*apartment*	в квартире
библиотека	*library*	в библиотеке
Дом	*house*	в доме
Кафе	*cafe*	в кафе
университет	*university*	в университете
Сад	*garden*	в саду
Лес	*forest*	в лесу

Please note that some words borrowed from foreign languages (such as **кафе** or **кино**) do not decline for cases, but foreign geographic locations (such as **Нью-Йорк**, **Лондон**, or **Париж**) do:

- **в Нью-Йорке** (*in New York*), **в Лондоне** (*in London*), **в Париже** (*in Paris*)

На (*at, on*)

Listen to Track 190

We use **на**:

1. When the object is located on some surface (the equivalent of English "on"):
   - Ваза стоит **на** подоконнике. – *The vase is standing **on** the windowsill.*
   - Учебник лежит **на** полке. – *The textbook is lying **on** the bookshelf.*

2. When the location is an open space or it used to be open in the past (the equivalent of English "at"):

   - Раньше мой отец работал **на** заводе. – *Earlier, my father worked **at** a plant.*

   - **На** Азиатском рынке в Москве можно купить разные экзотические продукты. – *One can buy different exotic foods **at** the Asian market in Moscow.*

Places that always require the preposition **на** are:

Listen to Track 191

Russian	**English**	**на + Prep. case**
Север	*north*	на севере
Юг	*south*	на юге
Запад	*west*	на западе
Восток	*east*	на востоке
Станция	*a small station (train, subway)*	на станции
Завод	*plant*	на заводе
Вокзал	*a large train station*	на вокзале
Концерт	*concert*	на концерте
Площадь	*square*	на площади
Работа	*work*	на работе
Улица	*street*	на улице
Рынок	*market*	на рынке
Почта	*post office*	на почте
Стадион	*stadium*	на стадионе

Other places/positions

Apart from **в** and **на**, the Russian language has plenty of other prepositions and adverbs that help describe an object's location. Adverbs don't impact the case of nouns, pronouns or adjectives, but prepositions put the words they go with into a certain case. We talked about it in detail in our chapter about Russian prepositions.

This table with examples illustrates how it works:

Listen to Track 192

Russian	English	Part of speech	Case	Example
над	*above, over*	Prep.	Instrumental	**Над** диваном висит книжная полка. *There's a bookshelf hanging **above** the sofa.*
под	*Under*	Prep.	Instrumental	Мой пес любит лежать **под** столом. *My dog loves lying **under** the table.*
Перед	*before, in front of*	Prep.	Instrumental	**Перед** нашим домом находится детская площадка. *There's a playground **in front of** our house.*
За	*behind, at*	Prep.	Instrumental	**За** столом сидят все мои близкие друзья. *All my close friends are sitting **at** the table.* Шкаф стоит **за** столом. *The wardrobe stands **behind** the table.*
Позади	*Behind*	Prep.	Accusative	Моя сестра сидит **позади** меня. *My sister is sitting **behind** me.*
около, возле	*by, near, next to*	Prep.	Genitive	**Около** моего офиса нет ни одного магазина. *There's not a single shop **near** my office.* Я живу **возле** станции метро Динамо. *I live **near** Dinamo subway station.*

у	*at, by*	Prep.	Genitive	Давай встретимся **у** входа в университет. *Let's meet **at** the university's main entrance.*
посреди	*in the middle*	Prep.	Genitive	**Посреди** площади всего несколько человек. *There are only a few people **in the middle of** the square.*
через дорогу	*across the street*	Prep. + noun	–	**Через дорогу** продаётся отличный латте. *They sell excellent latte **across the street**.*
здесь, тут	*Here*	Adverb	–	**Здесь** не курят. *No smoking in **here**.*
Там	*There*	Adverb	–	**Там** было очень много народу. ***There** were lots of people.*
близко	*Close*	Adverb	–	Я был очень **близко**, но не мог дотронуться. *I was very **close** but couldn't touch it.*
близко от	*close to*	Adverb + prep.	Genitive	Мы живём **близко от** центра города. *We live **close to** the city centre.*
Далеко	*Far*	Adverb	–	Озеро было **далеко**, и нам пришлось долго идти. *The lake was **far** away, and we had to walk for a long time.*

далеко от	*far from*	Adverb + prep.	Genitive	Моя бабушка живет **далеко от** станции метро. *My grandma lives **far from** the subway station.*
недалеко от	*not far from*	Prep.	Genitive	**Недалеко от** моей школы есть озеро. *There's a lake **not far from** my school.*
Внутри	*inside*	Adverb	–	Ключ находится **внутри** коробки. *The key is **inside** the box.*
снаружи	*outside, outdoors*	Adverb	–	Он попросил нас подождать **снаружи**. *He asked us to wait **outside**.*
Дома	*at home*	Adverb	–	В плохую погоду я предпочитаю оставаться **дома**. *In bad weather, I prefer to stay **at home**.*
наверху	*upstairs, up there, at the top*	Adverb	–	**Наверху** было много красивой мебели и картин. *There was lots of beautiful furniture and paintings **upstairs**.*
Внизу	*downstairs, below*	Adverb/ prep.	Accusative (for prep.)	Сегодня мне пришлось спать **внизу** на диване. *Tonight, I had to sleep **downstairs**, on a sofa.* Я забыл указать **внизу** свой адрес. *I forgot to write my address **below**.*

впереди	*ahead, ahead of, in front of*	Adverb/ prep.	Genitive (for prep.)	Ты иди **впереди**, а я за тобой. *You go **ahead**, and I will follow you.* **Впереди** нас едет красный автобус. *There's a red bus going **ahead of** us.*
Позади	*behind, past*	Adverb/ prep.	Genitive (for prep.)	Они пошли вперед и оставили нас далеко **позади**. *They went ahead and left us far **behind**.* **Позади** меня есть два свободных места. *There are two free seats **behind** me.*
Везде	*everywhere*	Adverb	–	Она **везде** ходит со своей подружкой. *She goes with her girlfriend **everywhere**.*
Нигде	*nowhere / anywhere*	Adverb	–	Я **нигде** не могу найти свой телефон. *I can't find my cell phone **anywhere**.*

Now you have a better idea of how to describe a position in Russian. Later, we will continue this topic and talk about the prepositions and adverbs that help you ask and give directions. Don't forget to check out our exercises and hone this topic to perfection.

TIME TO PRACTICE!

Exercise 1 - Fill in the gaps with the correct preposition (в or на):

1. _____ улице идет дождь. (*It's raining outside.*)
2. Миша работает хирургом _____ больнице. (*Misha works as a surgeon in a hospital.*)
3. _____ коробке было шесть булочек. (*There were six buns in the box.*)
4. _____ концертах в филармонии всегда много людей. (*There are always a lot of people at concerts in the Philharmonic Hall.*)
5. Сашу пригласили работать _____ телевидении. (*Sasha was invited to work on television.*)
6. Мы планируем провести выходные _____ домике _____ горах.(*We're planning to spend the weekend at a cabin in the mountains.*)

Exercise 2 - Fill in the table according to the preposition (в or на) these places go with. Put them into the prepositional case:

Концерт (concert), сад (garden), работа (work), музей (museum), вокзал (station), аптека (pharmacy), станция (station), стадион (stadium), парк (park), банк (bank), рынок (market), почта (post office), запад (west), кафе (café), больница (hospital), отель (hotel).

в	на

Exercise 3 - Put the nouns/pronouns in brackets into the correct case according to the preposition used:

1. Перед (моё окно) растет яблоня. (*An apple tree is growing in front of my window.*)

_____

2. Внизу (страница) нужно поставить подпись. (*At the bottom of the page you need to sign.*)

_____

3. Во время прогулки мы решили немного посидеть у (река). (*During the walk, we decided to sit by the river for a while.*)

_____

4. Мои родители живут недалеко от (мы). (*My parents live not far from us.*)

_____

5. Я устал, потому что просидел весь день за (компьютер). (*I'm tired because I've been sitting at the computer all day.*)

_____

6. Возле (вход) в магазин сидит пёс. (*Near the entrance to the store sits a dog.*)

_____

7. В детстве я любила прятаться от брата под (лестница). (*As a child, I used to hide under the stairs from my brother.*)

_____

Exercise 4 - Choose the most suitable question word or adverb of place:

1. (Внутри, снаружи, везде) было очень холодно, поэтому мы весь день оставались (внутри, нигде, дома). (*It was very cold ..., so we stayed ... all day.*)

_____

2. (Почем, где, сколько) продаются эти шоколадные батончики? (Тут, нигде, везде) в кафе или практически в любом супермаркете. (*... these chocolate bars sold? ... in a cafe or almost any supermarket.*)

_____

3. Он торопился, поэтому оставил меня одну (недалеко от, внутри, посреди) улицы и к тому же (рядом, далеко, наверху) от дома. (*He was in a hurry, so he left me alone ... the street and ... from home.*)

_____

4. (Недалеко, впереди, близко) от парка есть уютная кафешка, и (тут, там, здесь, везде) подают вкуснейший шоколадный чизкейк. (*... from the park there is a cozy cafe, and ... they serve delicious chocolate cheesecake.*)

_____

Answers

Exercise 1

1. На. 2. в. 3. В. 4. На. 5. на. 6. в, в.

Exercise 2

В	на
в саду	на концерте
в музее	на работе
в аптеке	на вокзале
в парке	на станции
в банке	на стадионе
в кафе	на рынке
в больнице	на почте
в отеле	на западе

Exercise 3

1. моим окном
2. страницы
3. реки
4. нас
5. компьютером
6. входа
7. лестницей

Exercise 4

1. Снаружи, дома
2. Где, тут
3. Посреди, далеко
4. Недалеко, там

Lesson 19: Russian Vocabulary for Daily Routines

From the early morning until the late evening, we live active lives full of different events. A great number of them are nothing special, just routine things that rarely make their way into our timetables (and never into our dairies). However, daily routine vocabulary is a key part of our everyday communication. So in this post, we will give you the words and phrases Russians use to describe their everyday actions. For your convenience, we divide them by the time of the day.

Morning Routine in Russian

Listen to Track 193

- **Просыпаться** – *wake up*
- **Вставать** – *get up*

  Я обычно встаю в шесть утра. – *I usually get up at six o'clock in the morning.*

  Во сколько ты обычно встаёшь? – *What time do you usually get up?*

  Я не люблю рано вставать, но мне приходится, потому что моя работа находится далеко от дома. – *I hate getting up early, but I have to because my work is far from home.*

- **Проспать** – *oversleep*
- **Опаздывать** – *be late*

  Я сегодня проспал и опоздал в школу. – *I overslept and was late for school.*

- **Выключать будильник** – *turn off the alarm clock*
- **Вставать с постели** – *get out of bed*
- **Заправлять постель** – *make the bed*

  Я люблю заправлять постель по утрам. Эта привычка помогает мне быть организованным. – *I love making the bed in the morning. This habit helps me stay organized.*

- **Идти в ванную** – *go to the bathroom*
- **Умываться** – *wash one's face*
- **Чистить зубы** – *brush one's teeth*
- **Когда я встаю, первым делом иду в ванную и умываюсь.** – *After I get up, I first go to the bathroom and wash my face.*

- **Затем я беру зубную щетку и зубную пасту и чищу зубы.** – *After that, I take my toothbrush and toothpaste and brush my teeth.*

- **Идти (выходить) на пробежку** – *go out for a jog*

  Каждое утро я иду на пробежку в парк. – *Every morning, I go out to the park for a jog.*

- **Утренняя пробежка** – *morning jog/run*

  Утренняя пробежка помогает мне взбодриться и поднимает настроение. – *A morning run energizes me and cheers me up.*

- **Делать зарядку (утреннюю гимнастику)** – *exercise*

- **Я всегда делаю утреннюю зарядку, чтобы чувствовать себя хорошо целый день.** – *I always do my morning exercises to feel well during the day.*

- **Принимать душ** – *take a shower*

- **После пробежки я всегда принимаю душ.** – *I always take a shower after the run.*

- **Причесываться** – *brush one's hair*

  Утром я причесываю себя и свою сестру. Она любит, когда я заплетаю ей косы. – *In the morning, I brush my hair and my sister's. She likes me to braid her hair.*

- **Делать макияж** – *put on makeup*

- **Мне нужно вставать пораньше, чтобы успеть сделать макияж.** – *I need to get up earlier to have enough time for the makeup.*

- **Моя сестра любит принимать душ по утрам.** – *My sister likes taking a shower in the morning.*

- **Одеваться** – *get dressed*

- **Одевать** – *get somebody dressed*

- **Собирать сумку/рюкзак** – *pack one's bag*

- **Готовить завтрак** – *make breakfast*

- **Пока моя мама готовит завтрак, я одеваюсь и собираю сумку.** – *While my mum makes me breakfast, I get dressed and pack my bag.*

- **Завтракать** – *have breakfast*

- **Я обычно завтракаю бутербродами и чаем.** – *I usually have sandwiches and tea for breakfast.*

- **Собирать ланчбокс** – *pack a lunch box*

- **Целовать/обнимать на прощание** – *kiss/hug goodbye*

- **Мама всегда обнимает и целует меня на прощание перед тем, как я ухожу.** – *My mum always hugs and kisses me goodbye before I leave.*
- **Обуваться** – *put on one's shoes*
- **Запирать дверь** – *lock the door*
- **Выходить из дома** – *leave the house*
- **Я всегда запираю дверь, прежде чем выйти из дома.** – *I always lock the door before leaving the house.*

In Russia, people always lock their doors when they go somewhere even if they just go to the shop nearby. Front doors in Russian homes have two or more locks and rest assured, Russian use all of them. Not that Russians are overly suspicious — it is rather a local standard of privateness (and safety).

Listen to Track 194

- **Садиться в машину** – *get in the car*
- **Идти на остановку** – *go to the bus stop*
- **Идти/ехать на работу** – *go to work*
- **Идти/ехать в школу (в университет)** – *go to school/university*
- **Идти/ехать на занятия** – *go to class*
- **Я обычно выхожу из дома в восемь, сажусь в машину и еду на работу.** – *I usually leave the house at eight, get in the car, and go to work.*
- **Завозить детей в школу** – *drive the kids to school*
- **Мы с мужем завозим детей в школу по очереди.** – *My husband and I drive the kids to school by turns.*
- **Начинаться** – *start*
- **Заканчиваться** – *finish, end*
- **Я еду в университет на метро. Занятия начинаются в девять, а заканчиваются в три.** – *I take the subway to my university. The classes start at nine and end at three in the afternoon.*

Afternoon routine in Russian

Listen to Track 195

- **Работать** – *work*
- **Я работаю каждый день с девяти до пяти.** – *I work every day from nine to five.*

- **Проверять электронную почту** – *check one's email*
- **Делать звонки** – *make phone calls*
- **Разговаривать по телефону** – *talk on the phone*
- **Отвечать на звонки** – *answer calls*
- **Проводить совещание** – *hold a meeting*
- **Встречаться с людьми** – *meet with people*
- **Стараться** – *do one's best*
- **Уставать** – *get tired*
- **Учиться** – *study*
- **Забирать ребенка (детей) со школы** – *pick the kid(s) up from school*
- **По дороге с работы я всегда забираю детей со школы и везу их на кружки.** – *On my way home from work, I always pick my kids up from school and drive them to other classes.*
- **Идти за покупками** – *go shopping*
- **Заезжать в магазин** – *stop by the store*
- **Покупать продукты** – *buy groceries*
- **Сегодня мне нужно заехать в магазин и купить некоторые продукты.** – *Today I need to stop by the store and buy some food.*
- **Готовить обед** – *make lunch*
- **Обедать** – *have lunch*
- **Я обычно обедаю с одногруппниками в университетской столовой.** – *I usually have lunch at the university canteen with my classmates.*
- **Кормить ребёнка/питомца** – *feed a child/pet*
- **Укладывать ребенка спать** – *put the child to sleep/nap*
- **Я кормлю ребенка и укладываю его спать, а потом у меня есть немного свободного времени.** – *I feed my child and put him to sleep, and then I have a little free time.*
- **Убираться (делать уборку)** – *clean (up)*
- **Стирать** – *do the laundry*
- **Гладить** – *iron*
- **Пылесосить** – *vacuum*
- **Вытирать пыль** – *dust*
- **Поливать комнатные растения** – *water the plants*
- **Помогать по дому** – *help around the house*

- **После школы я обычно помогаю маме по дому и убираюсь в своей комнате.** – *After school, I usually help my mum around the house and clean my room.*

Evening routine in Russian

Listen to Track 196

- **Возвращаться домой (с работы)** – *come back home (from work)*
- **Раздеваться** – *take off one's clothes*
- **Разуваться** – *take off one's shoes*
- **Переодеваться** – *change one's clothes*
- **Мыть руки с мылом** – *wash hands with soap*
- **Отдыхать** – *take a rest*
- **Читать книгу** – *read a book*
- **Слушать музыку** – *listen to music*
- **Идти на прогулку** – *go for a walk*
- **После работы я обычно немного отдыхаю. Лучший способ отдохнуть — это почитать книгу или сходить на прогулку.** – *After work, I usually take a rest. The best way to do it is to read a book or to go for a walk.*
- **Готовить ужин** – *make dinner*
- **Ужинать** – *have dinner*
- **Я всегда готовлю на ужин что-то особенное. Мы всегда ужинаем всей семьей.** – *I always make something special for dinner. We always have dinner together as a family.*
- **Мыть посуду** – *do the washing up*
- **Складывать посуду в посудомойку** – *load a dishwasher*
- **После ужина я не мою посуду. Я просто складываю ее в посудомойку и включаю.** – *I don't do the washing up after dinner. I just load the dishwasher and turn it on.*
- **Смотреть телевизор** – *watch TV*
- **Смотреть фильм/сериал** – *watch a movie/TV series*
- **Делать домашнее задание** – *do one's homework*
- **Составлять план на завтра** – *make plans for tomorrow*
- **Ходить в спортзал** – *go to the gym*
- **Тренироваться (заниматься спортом)** – *work out*

- **Общаться** – *hang out*
- **Проводить время вместе** – *spend time together*
- **Вечером я обычно встречаюсь со своими друзьями в спортзале. Мы вместе тренируемся и весело проводим время.** – *In the evening, I usually meet with my friends in the gym. We work out and have a great time together.*
- **Купаться** – *take a bath*
- **Принимать ванну** – *take a bath*
- **Ставить телефон на зарядку (заряжать телефон)** – *put the phone on a charger (charge a phone)*
- **Идти в постель (ложиться спать)** – *go to bed*
- **Заводить будильник** – *set an alarm clock*
- **Желать спокойной ночи** – *say good night*
- **Засыпать** – *fall asleep*
- **Я обычно ложусь спать очень поздно, после того, как сделаю все домашние дела.** – *I usually go to bed late at night after finishing all the chores.*
- **Перед тем, как ложиться спать, я завожу будильник на семь утра и желаю всем спокойной ночи.** – *Before going to bed, I set the alarm clock for 7 a.m. and say good night to everybody.*

Time expressions we use for daily routines

To talk about your everyday chores, you need to use some words for describing time frames. For example:

Listen to Track 197

- **Сначала** – *at first*
- **Потом** – *then*
- **После этого** – *after that*
- **Иногда** – *sometimes*
- **Часто** – *often*
- **Обычно** – *usually*
- **Поздно** – *late*
- **Рано** – *early*

- **Каждый день** – *every day*
- **По понедельникам** – *on Mondays*

It seems like you are now fully equipped for talking about your day. Knowledge is cool, but the practice is better. Take the time to think about your daily schedule and try to describe it using the phrases from our lesson. Our exercises will help you remember the vocabulary more easily and become more confident in talking about your daily routine. So jump in!

TIME TO PRACTICE!

Exercise 1 - Describe your morning routine in a few sentences in the present tense.

Example: Я обычно встаю в... (*I usually get up at...*) Первым делом я... (*The first thing I do is...*) Там я... (*There I...*) Потом я... (*Then I...*) После этого я... (*After that I...*)

_____

_____

_____

_____

Exercise 2 - Now describe your friend's (or family member's) afternoon routine (i.e., the time people usually spend outside their homes working, studying, etc.). You can use the words иногда (sometimes), часто (often), or обычно (usually).

_____

_____

_____

_____

Exercise 3- How does your family spend your evenings? What do you usually do? Describe your evening routine in a few sentences.

_____

_____

_____

_____

Exercise 4 - Fill the table with your daily activities by the day of the week. Follow our example:

По понедельникам	По вторникам	По средам	По четвергам	По пятницам	На выходных
Я обычно хожу в спортзал. (*I usually go to the gym*)					

Answers

Exercise 1

(example) Я обычно встаю в семь тридцать утра. Первым делом я заправляю постель и иду в ванную. Там я умываюсь, чищу зубы, и расчесываюсь. Потом я одеваюсь и делаю макияж. После этого я готовлю завтрак, ем, и еду на работу.

Exercise 2

(example) Егор работает в небольшой компании. Его рабочий день начинается в девять утра. Вначале он проверяет электронную почту и делает звонки, а потом встречается с разными людьми. Он обычно возвращается домой в пять вечера. Иногда по дороге с работы он заезжает в магазин купить продукты (еду).

Exercise 3

(example) Я обычно возвращаюсь домой со школы в три часа дня. Я мою руки, переодеваюсь и помогаю маме. Я прибираю в квартире или хожу за покупками. После этого мы вместе ужинаем. Потом я делаю домашнее задание. Если у меня есть свободное время, я читаю или слушаю музыку. Иногда ко мне вечером приходят друзья. Мы общаемся и отлично проводим время. Потом я принимаю душ, чищу зубы, завожу будильник и иду спать.

Exercise 4

(example)

По понедельникам	По вторникам	По средам	По четвергам	По пятницам	На выходных
Я обычно хожу в спортзал.	Я встречаюсь с друзьями.	Я много учусь.	Я помогаю маме и убираю в квартире.	Я хожу в кино	Я хожу за покупками.

Lesson 20: Asking and Telling About Directions in Russian

In our previous post, we explained how to ask and talk about an object's location. We also found out that the English word "where" is translated into Russian not only as **где** (asking about a location) but also as **куда** and **откуда** (asking about a direction). In this chapter, we will talk about these two words as well as about how to ask and give directions.

This topic is much broader than just navigating around the city when you get lost and ask a native for directions. Our everyday life is full of situations when we talk about directions. So we will start from the basic grammar that comes into action whenever an object changes its location.

Asking about directions

Listen to Track 198

If you are interested in where the object is moving to, start your question with **куда** (*where*):

- **Куда** едет этот трамвай? – *Where is this tram going?*

If you want to know where the object moves from, use **откуда** (where from):

- **Откуда** пришла посылка? – *__Where__ did the parcel come **from**?*

Откуда also has the meaning of a source and can even sometimes be translated as "*how*":

- **Откуда** ты знаешь о моей сестре?– *__How__ do you know my sister?*

Telling about directions

In our previous chapter about locations, we talked about the prepositions **в** (*in, at*) and **на** (*at, on*) that require the prepositional case. These prepositions can be used for directions as well, but with the only difference: we need to put them into the accusative case.

Listen to Track 199

For example,

- Я иду **в магазин**. – *I go **to the shop**.* (direction)

Compare it with:

- Я работаю **в магазине**. – *I work **at a shop**.* (location)

The same happens with **на:**

- В субботу мы едем **на дачу**. – *On Saturday, we **go to the dacha**.* (direction)
- Мои родители живут **на даче** все лето. – *My parents live **at the dacha** during the whole summer.* (location)

In our post on asking/talking about places, we gave you a list of places that can be used with either **в** or **на**. Nothing changes here for directions. The only difference is, again, the accusative case.

Listen to Track 200

For example:

- **Мы идем в театр (в аптеку, в кафе, в банк, в парк, в больницу, в школу…).**

But…

- **Мы едем на стадион (на север, на станцию, на концерт, на площадь, на работу, на рынок…).**
  We're going to the stadium (to the north, to the station, to the concert, to the square, to work, to the market…)

Other prepositions and adverbs of direction

Russian has tons of ways to describe directions. We have collected them in one table to help you see how they are used and what cases are required for each of them.

Listen to Track 201

Russian	English	Part of speech	Case	Example
с	from, down	Prep.	Genitive	Ехать на велосипеде **с** горки всегда легче, чем на горку. *Riding a bike **down** the hill is always easier than doing it up the hill.*
Из	from (inside), out of	Prep.	Genitive	Вчера отец учил меня выезжать на машине **из** гаража. *Yesterday, my dad taught me to drive **out of** the garage.*
из-за	from behind	Prep.	Genitive	Солнце выглянуло **из-за** туч. *The sun peeked out **from behind** the clouds.*
из-под	from under, from beneath, from underneath	Prep.	Genitive	Он достал **из-под** подушки книгу и начал читать. *He pulled a book **from under** a pillow and started to read.*
Вдоль	along	Prep.	Genitive	Идите **вдоль** берега реки, пока не увидите мост. *Walk **along** the river shore until you see a bridge.*
к(о)	to, towards	Prep.	Dative	Подойди **ко** мне. *Come **to** me.*
По	along, by, on, in, through	Prep.	Dative	Мы шли **по** берегу **по** песку, а дети бежали рядом **по** траве. *We were walking **in** the sand **along** the shore, and the kids were running **through** the grass nearby.*

Под	under	Prep.	Accusative	Положи тетрадь **под** книгу. *Put the notebook **under** the book.*
Через	over, through, across	Prep.	Accusative	Чтобы выйти на дорогу, вам нужно переплыть **через** ручей и пройти **через** лес. *To get on the road, you need to swim **across** the stream and walk **through** the forest.*
Сквозь	through	Prep.	Accusative	Солнце светило **сквозь** штору. *The sun was shining **through** the curtain.*
За	behind	Prep.	Accusative	Луна спряталась **за** гору и стало темно. *The moon hid **behind** the mountain and it got dark.*
Вокруг	around, round	Adverb / Prep.	Genitive for prep.	Задание было пробежать **вокруг** школы три раза. *The task was to run **around** the school three times.*
Мимо	past	Adverb / Prep.	Genitive for prep.	По дороге на работу я всегда прохожу **мимо** булочной. *On my way to work, I always go **past** the bakery.*
Вверх	up, upwards	Adverb	–	Чтобы попасть ко мне в офис, нужно подняться **вверх** на лифте на двенадцатый этаж. *To get into my office, you need to take the elevator **up** to the twelfth floor.*
Наверх	up, upstairs, upward, to the top	Adverb	–	Поднимись **наверх** и жди меня там. *Go **upstairs** and wait for me there.*

Вниз	down, downstairs	Adverb	—	Когда я смотрю **вниз** с десятого этажа, у меня кружится голова. *When I look **down** from the tenth floor, I get dizzy.* Уборная находится **вниз** по лестнице. *The WC is **downstairs**.*
Прямо	straight ahead	Adverb	—	Идите **прямо**, потом поверните налево. *Go **straight ahead**, then turn to the left.*
Вперед	forward, ahead (of), on(ward)	Adverb	—	Туристы продолжали продвигаться **вперед**, несмотря на дождь. *The tourists kept moving **forward** despite the rain.*
Назад	back(wards)	Adverb	—	Мечта тянет меня **вперед**, а сомнения — **назад**. *The dream pulls me **forward** while my doubts hold me **back**.* Назад и вперед—*back and forth*.
Направо	to the right	Adverb	—	На следующем перекрестке поверните, пожалуйста, **направо**. *At the next intersection, turn **to the right**, please.*
Налево	to the left	Adverb	—	Здесь надо повернуть **налево**. *You need to turn **to the left** here.*
Сюда	here	Adverb	—	Посмотри **сюда**! *Look **here**!*

Туда	there	Adverb	–	Дорожный указатель показывает, что надо повернуть **туда**. *The road sign shows we need to turn **there**.*
на север (юг, восток, запад)	north (south, east, west)	Adverb	–	Дорога идет **на север**, а потом поворачивает **на восток**. *The road goes **north** and then turns **east**.*

We hope you now have a better idea of how to talk about directions in Russian. But how about real situations? For example, imagine that...

You got lost and ask a native for a direction

What would you say? Let's look at the phrases that may help you to explain your situation and ask for help. (Note that we give these phrases in the polite form since you are talking to a stranger.)

Listen to Track 202

Я потерялся / Я потерялась.	*I got lost.*
Скажите, пожалуйста, где я сейчас?	*Tell me please, where am I now?*
Какая это улица?	*What street is this?*
Мне нужно на Красную площадь.	*I need to go to Red Square.*
Как отсюда попасть в Кремль?	*How do I get to the Kremlin from here?*
Как отсюда добраться до Большого театра?	*How do I get to Bolshoi Theatre from here?*
Простите, не подскажете, как мне пройти к парку Горького?	*Excuse me, could you please tell me how I get to Gorky Park?*
Извините, где здесь уборная?	*Excuse me, where is the WC?*
Где здесь поблизости кафе или ресторан?	*Where is a cafe nearby?*
Это далеко? Это недалеко?	*Is it far? Is it near?*
Туда можно дойти пешком?	*Can I go there on foot?*
Подскажите, пожалуйста, где здесь ближайшая станция метро?	*Could you please tell me where the nearest subway station is?*
Где здесь ближайшая остановка автобуса (трамвая, троллейбуса)?	*Where is the nearest bus (tram, trolleybus) stop?*
Куда едет этот поезд (автобус)?	*Where is this train (bus) going?*
Покажите мне, пожалуйста, на карте.	*Please show me on the map.*

How to give directions in Russian

If you know how to give directions, there will be no problem understanding someone else's instructions. Who knows, maybe one day you'll have to save a Russian tourist from getting lost in your country :)

Here are the basic phrases that help direct a person to the right place.

Listen to Track 203

Куда вам нужно?	*Where do you need to go?*
Это далеко / недалеко.	*It's far. / It's not far.*
Пешком очень далеко.	*It's too far to go on foot.*
Минут десять пешком.	*It's ten minutes on foot.*
Можно дойти пешком.	*You can go on foot.*
Идите прямо до магазина.	*Go straight ahead to the shop.*
Перейдите через дорогу / площадь.	*Cross the road/square.*
Потом поверните направо / налево.	*Then turn to the right/left.*
Заверните за угол.	*Turn around the corner.*
Идите по этой улице.	*Go along this street.*
Вам нужно сесть на автобус номер 305.	*You need to take bus number 305.*
Это далеко. Вам лучше сесть на маршрутное такси или автобус.	*It is far from here. You'd better take a taxi or bus.*
Остановка вон там, возле Макдональдса.	*The bus stop is over there, near the MacDonald's.*
Ближайшая станция метро в двух минутах ходьбы.	*The nearest subway station is a two-minute walk.*
Поверните направо на следующем перекрестке.	*Turn to the right at the next intersection.*
Вам нужно вернуться немного назад.	*You need to go back a little.*

At this point, you may feel like a navigation ninja, or ... like you are completely lost in these directions. Don't worry. Just like any other topic, this one also requires some time to practice, and it's better to do it in real life. Don't worry if you mess something up. A kind smile will get you further than any words!

TIME TO PRACTICE!

Exercise 1 - Fill in the gaps with the correct prepositions (в / на) and put the underlined nouns/adjectives in the correct case:

1. С утра мне нужно было зайти (в / на) <u>аптека</u>, а потом бежать (в / на) <u>работа</u>. (*In the morning I had to go to the pharmacy, and then run to work.*)

   _____

2. До того, как моего брата пригласили работать (в / на) <u>крупная строительная компания</u>, он пробовал устроиться (в / на) <u>завод</u>. (*Before my brother was invited to work for a large construction company, he tried to get a job in a factory.*)

   _____

3. Летом я планирую поступить (в / на) <u>университет</u> и переехать (в / на) <u>Москва</u>. (*In the summer, I plan to go to university and move to Moscow.*)

   _____

4. Завтра мои друзья идут (в / на) <u>концерт</u> (в / на) <u>театр</u> и меня с собой зовут. (*Tomorrow my friends are going to a concert at the theater, and I'm invited to go with them.*)

   _____

5. Предлагаю сейчас одеться и пойти (в / на) <u>парк</u>.(*I suggest you get dressed now and go to the park.*)

   _____

Exercise 2 - Fill in the gaps with the correct question word (куда / откуда) and put the underlined nouns/adjectives in the case the preposition requires:

1. (Куда / Откуда) выглянуло солнце? Оно выглянуло из-за <u>облако</u>. (*Where did the sun come from? It peeked out from behind the clouds.*)

   _____

2. (Куда / Откуда) мне идти? Иди к <u>учитель</u>. (*Where should I go? Go to the teacher.*)

   _____

3. (Куда / Откуда) упало яблоко? Оно упало с <u>дерево</u>.(*Where did the apple fall from? It fell from a tree.*)

   _____

4. (Куда / Откуда) выехала машина? Она выехала из <u>парковка</u>. (*Where did the car come from? It pulled out of the parking lot.*)

   _____

5. (Куда / Откуда) поставить коробку? Поставь ее под <u>стол</u>. (*Where should I put the box? Put it under the table.*)

   _____

Exercise 3 - Imagine that you get lost on the street and ask a native for help. Put the dialogue phrases into the correct order:

— Добрый день!

_____

— Пожалуйста.

_____

— Перейдите через площадь и возле того памятника поверните налево.

_____

— Вам лучше проехаться на метро.

_____

— Не подскажете, где здесь ближайшая станция?

_____

— Мне нужно в музей космонавтики, я правильно иду?

_____

— Спасибо большое!

_____

— Она недалеко, три минуты пешком.

_____

— Это далеко отсюда.

_____

— Здравствуйте. Чем могу помочь?

_____

— Идите вдоль улицы, и там вы увидите станцию метро.

Exercise 4 - Translate these phrases into Russian using the imperative mood (the form of instruction) following the example:

English	Russian
turn to the left	поверните налево
cross the road	
walk along the street	
turn around the corner	
go upstairs	
go past the pharmacy	
run here	
drive out of the parking	

Answers

Exercise 1

1. в аптеку, на работу
2. в крупной строительной компании, на завод
3. в университет, в Москву
4. на концерт, в театр
5. на улицу, в парк

Exercise 2

1. Откуда, из-за облака
2. Куда, к учителю
3. Откуда, с дерева
4. Откуда, из парковки
5. Куда, под стол

Exercise 3

— Добрый день!
— Здравствуйте. Чем могу помочь?
— Мне нужно в музей космонавтики, я правильно иду?
— Это далеко отсюда.
— Вам лучше проехаться на метро.
— Не подскажете, где здесь ближайшая станция?
— Она недалеко, три минуты пешком. Перейдите через площадь и возле того памятника поверните налево. Идите вдоль улицы, и там вы увидите станцию метро.
— Спасибо большое!
— Пожалуйста.

Exercise 4

English	Russian
turn to the left	поверните налево
cross the road	перейдите дорогу
walk along the street	идите вдоль улицы
turn around the corner	заверните за угол
go upstairs	поднимитесь вверх по ступенькам
go past the pharmacy	идите мимо аптеки
come here	подойдите сюда
drive out of the parking	выезжайте из парковки

Conclusion

Learning grammar is never an easy task, so if you were able to finish all the lessons in this book by consistently learning everyday, kudos to you. You did an amazing job, and you should be very happy with your achievement.

If you were not able to follow the daily schedules recommended, don't despair. The important thing is you made use of this book to build a solid foundation for your Russian grammar. We at My Daily Russian hope that you will continue to keep learning everyday.

Even just an hour a day or less will go a long way. It could be just listening to a 30-minute Russian podcast, watching a Russian movie or TV series, writing to a friend in Russian, talking to a native Russian speaker, changing your social media settings to Russian or reading the news in Russian ... the list goes on.

If you wish to further your studies in Russian language, we have other books available at My Daily Russian and on Amazon. Please feel free to browse the different titles. The books such as Russian Short Stories will help improve your reading and listening skills as well as solidify the knowledge you have learned in this grammar book.

Thank you so much for using this book. It has been a great 20 days (or more) with you. We wish you the best of luck in your Russian studies.

Thank you,

My Daily Russian Team

Instructions on How to Download the Audio

Please take note that the audio are in MP3 format and need to be accessed online. No worries though; it's quite easy!

On your computer, smartphone, iphone/ipad or tablet, simply go to this link:

https://mydailyrussian.com/audio-grammar-beginner/

Do you have any problems downloading the audio? If you do, feel free to send an email to support@mydailyrussian.com. We'll do our best to assist you, but we would greatly appreciate if you could thoroughly review the instructions first.

Thank you.

Printed in Great Britain
by Amazon

15380010R00127